The Book of Seasons

A Search for our Rural Roots

by

Pamela Newton

Author of "The Cape Breton Book of Days"

Illustrations by Peter Gamble

GREENFIELD PUBLISHING

"Song of the Open Road" from *VERSES FROM 1929* by Ogden Nash. Copyright 1932 by Ogden Nash. By permission of Little, Brown and Company.

"Two Tramps in Mud Time" from THE POETRY OF ROBERT FROST EDITED BY EDWARD CONNERY LATHEM, Copyright 1936 by Robert Frost, © 1964 by Lesley Frost Ballantine, © 1969 by Henry Holt and Company, Inc. Reprinted by permission of Henry Holt and Company, Inc.

Items on Mummering are reprinted (or quoted) from the article *"Christmas Customs"* by Wayne C Stockwood, *ENCYCLOPEDIA OF NEWFOUNDLAND AND LABRADOR*, Volume One, First Edition, 1967, St. John's with the kind permission of the Joseph R. Smallwood Heritage Foundation Inc.

Cover photograph - "Cutting hay on the bluff at Ingonish Beach © 1910, Cabot Archives at the Beaton Institute, U.C.C.B., Sydney, N.S.

Cover Design: Harve Grant

Published by Greenfield Publishing

PO Box 512 North Sydney. Nova Scotia. B2A 3M5.

Canadian Cataloguing in Publication Data

Newton, Pamela, 1939-

The book of seasons

ISBN 0969912307

1. Seasons. 2. Country life. I. Gamble, Peter. II. Title.

GR930.N48 1997 398.23'6 C97-950204-7

Printed by City Printers, Sydney. N.S.

"The farther we get away from the land, the greater our insecurity."
- Henry Ford

"To every thing there is a season, and a time to every purpose under the heaven:"
- Ecclesiastes 3:1

"The prepared roots of potatoes...stop flux of the bowels and nourish much...and then increase seed and provoke Lust, causing Fruitfulness in both sexes."
Herbal advice circa, 1710.

Dedicated to my husband, David,
and to my children -
Elizabeth, Michael, Christopher, Sandra, Laura Jane, and Andrew.

Preface

The farm on which we live has been farmed since Cape Breton Island was opened for settlement in 1785. It was originally granted to Joseph Jefferson, a Loyalist from Virginia.

About 100 years ago the Jefferson family still lived and farmed here. Their children were about the same ages as my children. One difference, however, was that the Jeffersons, like many rural families, had an older relative living with them. Their neighbours were other Loyalists as well as settlers from England. Today, our neighbours are mostly descendents of those early settlers, although there are "people from away". I am from New York City and my ancestors were Patriots, not Loyalists, during the Revolutionary War but my husband, David, is a settler from England, so there is a pattern.

Today a tractor and modern farming equipment have taken the place of the Jeffersons' horses and simple equipment. We have a car instead of a buggy and sleigh. There are still horses on the farm, but they are used for pleasure, not for work.

We grow no buckwheat, barley or oats, but continue to grow potatoes. Once we raised sheep and cattle, and where the Jeffersons raised about a dozen sheep and a few cows, we had at one time some two hundred sheep and twenty head of beef. Today our plastic covered greenhouses and the modern hydroponic growing system would have been something out of science fiction for the Jeffersons. Our main crops of tomatoes, hot peppers, pickling cukes and flowers would also have been considered frivolous by them.

The years have passed, farming methods have changed, and our way of life is different. But the land, the family, the seasons remain unchanged, and this book explores seasonal rituals which have embedded themselves in our lives and made an indelible imprint upon us.

I wish to thank Peter Gamble for all the help he has given me in the preparation of suitable sketches which have so enhanced the book.

I also wish to thank Kate Currie and the Beaton Institute, Helen Ballah Dunn of North Sydney, Rita Joe of Eskasoni, Mildred Lewis of Point Edward, Mary Jane MacIsaac of Glendyer, Alastair MacLeod of Point Edward, Jack MacDonald of Sydney, Ada and Alex MacLean of McKinnon Harbour, Elizabeth MacNaughton of St. Patrick's Channel, George MacNeil of Bay St Lawrence and Sydney, and Donald Walker of Ottawa Brook for their help and their invaluable memories, and Wilfred MacLean and my daughter, Elizabeth, as well as the Bridgewater, Nova Scotia library for help in searching out information.

For their assistance in tracking down photos and illustrations I thank Pam and Scott Andrews, Bill Craig, Peg Cummings,

Owen Fitzgerald, Colleen Kosick, Margery MacInnis, Lynne Moore, my daughter Sandra, the Nova Scotia Archives, Jim O'Brien, Janice Peters, Donald Robb, Peter Sanger, John Sobel, Charles Thompson, Charles and Jan Van Nostrand, and Fred Williams and the Cabot Archives.

I also wish to thank my daughter, Laura Jane, for her help with the manuscript and my husband David for his patience and time.

While most of the places mentioned are located on Cape Breton Island, where I live in Nova Scotia, the story has relevance for all of us, wherever we live, be it in the city or country.

Introduction

Most people live in cities, towns or suburbs, far removed from a rural way of life. Some may never been have in the country while others have memories limited to visiting grandfather's farm as children in the summers - warm memories of picking potatoes and helping to make hay. Today, many people are unable to return to grandfather's farm so they are drawn by nostalgia or curiosity to agricultural exhibitions or just to the local park to feed the ducks. Others simply drive through the countryside in autumn to see the fall colours of the leaves. There is something different about the country. We feel freer, less stressed, and find pleasant spots to daydream. In recent years there has been a marked increase in recreational walking. Is this an instinctive effort to disengage from the highly technological life of today? Is it a quiet confirmation that we are connected to nature and need to be closer to it for our physical, mental and spiritual health?

People in towns and cities have gardens, flower beds and grass and there are trees and parks outside. Inside, they have houseplants and flowers. In some areas, a high value is placed on the number of parks in a city where they are considered a factor in a better quality of life. They are called "the lungs of the city", because they cleanse both the air and the human spirit.

For many of us life in the good old days seems to have been simpler. There was a different outlook on life and people were happier.

But memories of a way of life in the good old days back at grandfather's farm are perhaps not exactly how things were. Yes, life was simpler. It was also harder.

There was a rhythm to their lives. People had purpose. In the good old days, our forefathers knew what they had to do. There was a personal responsibility. There was hard work, and if they didn't do their part they affected the family and its survival. If they had to bring in firewood in a storm and didn't want to go out in the storm and get cold and wet, they did it anyway - or the fire would go out. They pushed hard. They went the "extra mile". They relied on themselves, their family, their neighbours. They had responsibility and for most that meant they also had integrity. Life was hard but rewarding. People had skills. They could grow a good potato, build a farm gate, deliver a lamb, and put their hand to just about anything. When times were hardest, there was help and there was support.

The rhythm of the seasons made the rhythm of life. In rural areas people are physically closer to nature. If they are farmers, their lives and livelihood - whether it is growing a crop, or raising livestock - depend on nature and revolve with the seasons of the year.

Seasons are a way we mark time passing. They dictate our behaviour - how we dress, our activities. Seasons may also trigger old ways of doing things, stir ancient and dormant memories. When faced with certain situations we respond much like our forefathers. Today we still revel in a spring morning, feel good on a summer day, and huddle by a flickering fire for warmth and comfort on a cold snowy evening. We even prefer to sit around that fire, though our central heating has made it redundant.

This book is about seasons. It is a memory book of life. Some memories are personal, some belong to others, most are shared by all.

The rhythms of life on a farm are unchanged, although some of the ways in which we respond to those rhythms have changed. We now have all kinds of labour-saving devices in the home and a wide variety of farm equipment to help with the chores of farming. There is instant communication and limitless information. But we remain connected to our past because snow still has to be shovelled and spring mud is still muddy and hay still needs to be made while the sun shines.

There is also a rhythm to the seasons and there is a rhythm to our daily lives although the ancient rhythms are being deluged in a cacophany of modern sound. Some things had to be done every day - meals fixed, children tended, cows milked. Specific tasks were done on specific days. Monday was wash day. Tuesday was for ironing. On Wednesday we baked. Thursday was the day for scrubbing upstairs and for changing the beds. Friday brought us downstairs to scrub the kitchen, pantry, parlor and porch. Saturday was extra busy. We baked again. And we got all ready for Sunday. On Sunday all we could do was to go to church, and visit with friends and neighbours. We couldn't work. Only essential livestock chores were permitted and the washing of the midday dinner dishes. Everything else was done the day before - wood brought in, kindling cut, meat and vegetables cooked and put in the pot - already to be heated up. Sunday was a day of rest.

Spring

MARCH/APRIL/MAY

March is the traditional beginning of spring. But here in the Maritimes it is more like the continuation of winter with cold, storms and snow.

Even April is not spring for the storms, snow and raw cold continue.

Yet signs of spring are appearing. By May there may still be snow, particularly in the woods. The wind blows from the North over ice floes packed into our harbours, and the ground can ring hard with frost. Yet we also see green grass, the beginnings of flowers and budding on the trees and a promise of summer.

"And the spring comes slowly up this way."

by Samuel Coleridge

MARCH

March is a harsh month named for Mars, the Roman god of War. Mars, the warrior, had many festivals held in the spring, because that was the start of the season for military campaigns. So Mars' name was given to the first month of the old Roman year.

Mars was also an agricultural god, the protector of the fields against disease and weather in times of peace as well as in war.

The month has been called *"March many-weathers"*. In Gaelic it is *"Mart" or "Earrach Geamradh"* - *"the Winter Month"*. In Celtic *"Lentzinmanoth"* - *"Renewal Month"*, and in Micmac *"Si'Ko'Ku's"* - *"the Breaking of Winter"*. The full moon was the *"Worm"* or *"Sap Moon"*.

If March comes in like a lion it will go out like a lamb, or vice versa.

Like an army defeated
The snow hath retreated.
"March" by William Wordsworth.

Today in March we too sometimes feel like warriors, battling the long winter.

The reasons for some beliefs are lost in antiquity. For example, a windy and a dry March was said to be good for corn, and a wet March made a sad harvest. Perhaps it was because a dry March allowed the soil to warm more quickly in the following months and farmers to seed earlier. But why was it also said that a windy and dry March was evil for old folk and child-bearing women?

The first holiday of the month is March 17, St. Patrick's Day. It falls in mid-March, the time of the year in Ireland when herds go out to pasture and crops are planted. Many legends have developed around St. Patrick. He had great influence and he said that if a king ruled well his reign would bring good weather, calm seas, and abundant crops. But if he ruled badly, then his reign would bring bad weather and the failure of crops.

St. Patrick's birthplace is disputed, but not his capture at age sixteen when he was taken by pirates to Ireland as a slave. A swineherd before he escaped, he entered a monastery and eventually, after much travel, returned to Ireland as a bishop to spread the word of Christianity.

His greatest enemies were the Druid priests, considered very powerful magicians. But Patrick had his own magic. Legend has it that to destroy the Druids he was compelled to curse their fertile lands, making them into bogs; curse their rivers so they didn't produce any fish; curse their kettles so that no amount of fire could make them boil; and curse the Druid priests themselves so that the earth was said to open and swallow them.

The legend of his ridding Ireland of snakes can be related to his destroying its pagan gods and priests. True or false, to this day there are no snakes in Ireland. Nor any Druid priests.

The shamrock, the three leaved small white clover (trifolium repens), has been connected to St. Patrick. He may have used it to explain the concept of the Trinity. However, it is curious that the trefoil in Arabic was called the shamrakh, and was held sacred in Iran as symbolic of the Persian Triads. In his Natural History, the ancient Roman Pliny wrote that serpents were never seen on trefoil, and it prevailed against the sting of snakes and scorpions.

Today St. Patrick's Day is celebrated with much use of the colour green. People wear green clothes, carry green shamrocks and drink green beer. Spring is coming and green is the colour of the new growth of nature. Ireland itself is so green that it is called the Emerald Isle.

Spring Equinox is the first official day of spring, the changeover point between the dark and the light halves of the year. The sun rises due east and sets due west and gives exactly twelve hours of daylight and twelve hours of darkness.

If on that day the wind is from the west, they said, we will have a fine summer, if it comes from the south, it will be wet.

Fishermen did not like to go out around the time of the Equinox. There was always fear of a large storm. If the sun crosses the Equinox line with a northeast wind and a snowstorm, there will be three months of bad weather, they said. But if the weather is good, there will be a fine spring. Some fishermen satirically called the spring storm "Gentle Annie", although this is a corruption of "Anu", the Celtic goddess connected with the coming of spring. In Newfoundland this storm is called "Sheilah's Brush".

How do we know it's spring? There are several signs and several ways of interpreting them. The first robin sighted; winter supplies are depleted and stored potatoes have extra long eyes. As the snow melts, spring tides and rivers rise higher than usual, forcing their way through banks and dykes, causing considerable damage.

Deer come out of the woods and frequent the fields. Spring is here when the snow has melted enough for you to plant your foot on bare ground or on nine daisies.

The ponds must freeze over three times in the spring before you hear the frogs sing. A frog that opens its mouth in March will close it in April. That frog has started to sing before it really is spring.

Kittens born in March are reported to be the best kind for keeping.

I wandered lonely as a cloud
That floats on high o'er vales and hills,
When all at once I saw a crowd,
A host of golden daffoldils;
Beside the lake, beneath the trees,
Fluttering and dancing in the breeze...

For oft, when on my couch I lie
In vacant or in pensive mood,
They flash upon that inward eye
Which is the bliss of solitude;
And then my heart with pleasure fills,
And dances with the daffoldils.

Daffoldils by William Wordsworth

March is the best time for "spring chickens" to hatch.

There has been a long tradition of the relationship between chickens and people. Chickens are raised for both their eggs and their meat. Some of the ancient Romans preceded modern agriculture techniques by raising roosters in small cages. To fatten them they were fed wheat bread soaked in wine or milk.

Chickens can be used medicinally. The old favorite - chicken soup for colds - has been found by scientists to be valid.

There is supposed to be a difference between the broth made from a young hen or pullet and that of an old bird.

The broth of a fat hen was used, among other things, for leprosy. From a young rooster it was good for stopping dysentary but, surprisingly, that of an old bird was recommended as a laxative. Best to know what age your bird was! The broth of an old rooster was also used for headaches, nausea and for asthma. Cream of chicken soup was believed good for those suffering from stomach ulcers.

A popular remedy for arthritis was the wing bone of a hen bored through with a spoon, tied with thread in seven knots, and held over the swollen portion of the body.

The brain of a hen was considered useful in stopping nosebleeds. And the grease or fat of a hen was believed to cure chapped lips and pains in the ears.

And even if you don't use chickens medicinally, you have been involved with them since childhood. Think of the famous chickens in stories.

Remember the Little Red Hen, the hardworking hen? Whenever she asks the other lazy barnyard animals to help sow the wheat or reap, thresh, mill or bake it into bread, they all refused *"Not I, Not I"*. *"Then I will do it myself"*, said the Little Red Hen - and she did.

Chicken Little is, of course, the flighty bird who thinks the sky is falling, when something falls on her head. *"Oh dear me,"* she cries. *"The sky is falling. I must go and tell the King."*

Here's a hen I'd like to have:

I had a little hen, the prettiest ever seen
She washed me the dishes and kept the house clean.
She baked me my bread, she brewed me my ale
She sat by the fire and told many a fine tale.

And who can forget the chicken who wants to cross the road?

There's also a long tradition that every farmer goes to bed with the chickens at dusk and gets up with the crowing of the rooster at dawn.

Many believed that their chickens would be like the first person who came to the house on New Year's Day. If a stout, prosperous person, then you'd have plump chickens.

If a hen runs into the house, it's not necessarily because you left the door open. It may be that someone is coming to visit. Colours of hens make a difference. If a red hen crows, for example, it means there will be a fire; if a black hen crows, there will be good weather, and a white hen means good luck.

People take on the characteristics of chickens. You can look as dejected as a plucked chicken or be madder than a wet hen. You might be as fussy as a mother hen, or as proud as a hen with one chick (a hen with one chick often seems more anxious and possessive than a hen with a dozen).

Have you ever said "there's no one here but us chickens" or "we're as sociable as chickens in a coop"? And once the pecking order is established, chickens are sociable.

How many times have you run around like a chicken with its head cut off? Maybe your handwriting looks like chicken scratches, and your children think their allowances are mere chicken feed.

Chick or chickabiddy is a term of endearment for a child. And chick and spring chicken have been used to describe a young woman. A hen, except for a mothering hen, is generally used in an uncomplimentary sense with reference to older women - "She's no chicken; she's on the wrong side of 30" said one undiplomatic male and "hen" often refers to aggressive or meddling women. So a henhouse was once widely used to describe a house controlled by a woman. A hen party summons up the picture of gossiping females, and henpecked is perhaps the most widely used term applied to a husband who is dominated by his wife.

A cowardly person might be chicken-hearted or chicken-livered. The word chicken is used to describe a coward, but this is strange because the rooster is a symbol of bravery while the mother hen, if anything, exceeds him in courage when she defends her chicks.

You can look like a chicken and feel like a chicken, but don't count your chickens before they hatch..

> To make a cock ale: *"Take 8 gallons of ale; then take a March cock and boil him well; and take 4 pounds of raisins, 2 or 3 nutmegs, 3 or 4 flakes of mace and l/2 pound dates. Beat all these in a mortar, and add to them 2 quarts of the best sherry-sack. Put all this into the ale, with the cock and stop it close for 6 or 7 days, and then bottle it; and after a month you may drink it."* (1669 cookbook)

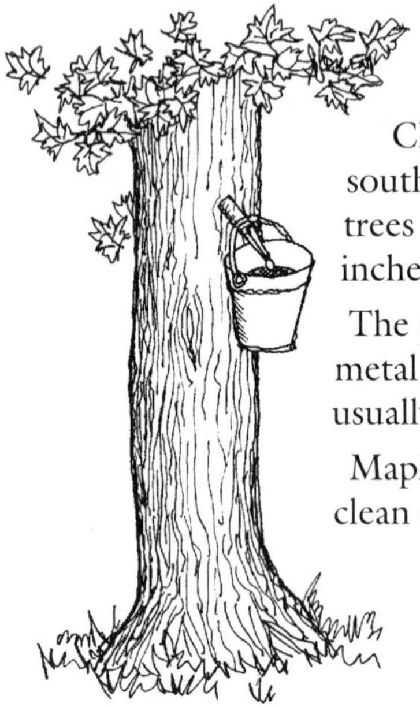

Spring is maple sugaring time, when the days get warmer and the nights remain frosty. Chipmunks are seen by the walls or the woodpile. All a person has to do is wait for the sap to rise. A south or a southeast wind is beneficial when the collecting starts. It takes about forty quarts of sap of maple trees to make one quart of syrup. This is the amount of sap that comes from an average maple tree (twelve inches in diameter) during the entire spring season.

The procedure is fairly simple. You bore a three inch hole into a sugar maple, pull out the bit and insert a metal or wooden spigot, hang a bucket or other container on the spigot and let nature drip away. The sap will usually run for a month.

Maple syrup is popular with pancakes, but it is also good with a variety of other foods. Pouring the syrup on clean snow is an "ice cream" treat.

The moon has always played an important role in our lives. In ancient times it was worshipped, but even in more recent times, farmers did certain chores according to the phases of the moon. The waning moon, when the moon was decreasing, was a good time to plough, plant certain crops, and harvest, because it was believed that the natural juices of all things were also on the wane. It was not a good time to butcher because the meat would be drier and tasteless, willow or birch cut for hoops or baskets would not be supple, pine trees cut for building would become too brittle. It was a good time for firewood cutting and just before the new moon was the best time to lay floors amd roof shingles. Animals were gelded (castrated) in the wane, and eggs laid in the wane were used for hatching. Birds hatched in the moon's increase were said to be difficult to raise.

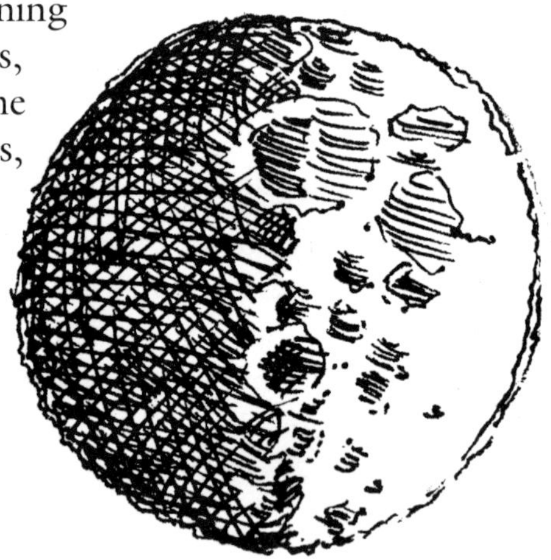

The waxing moon, when the moon is increasing, was a propitious time to get married and a good time to cut sap wood for barrels.

The crescent moon was a popular and beneficial time to start on a journey or undertake any new task.

The moon can be a guide for those who travel at night. It follows the same sky route as the sun - from east to west. A line drawn through the horns of a crescent moon generally indicates north and south. A waxing crescent moon rises at sunset and follows closely behind the setting sun, while a waning crescent, rises in the east just ahead of the sun. The full moon is always directly opposite the sun, so a person can orient himself.

It was believed that children and animals born in the full moon were larger and stronger than those born in the wane. Springborn animals were supposed to grow better. Much of this belief makes sense as the pasture was just beginning to grow, there was ample milk from their mothers.

It was said that if a baby boy is born in the wane of the moon, the next child will be a girl and vice versa. When a baby is born in the increasing moon, the next child will be the same sex.

One legend has it that a man collecting firewood on a Sunday was banished to the moon. According to a Scandanavian legend, the moon kidnapped two children, Hjuki and Bil, who had been drawing water suspended from a pole. The children, pole and bucket were put up on the moon, where they could be seen from earth.

Hjuki and Bil became our Jack and Jill. The fall of Jack and the subsequent fall of Jill represent the vanishing of one moon spot after another as the moon wanes, as it decreases.

Hjuki comes from the word to heap or pile together and increase, and Bil from bila, to break up or dissolve. So Hjuki and Bil, Jack and Jill, are the waxing and waning of the moon. And the water they carry is the rainfall, infuenced by the phases of the moon.

Jack and Jill went up the hill,
To fetch a pail of water;
Jack fell down, and broke his crown,
And Jill came tumbling after.

The cutting and uses of wood dominated all rural life, the further north on this continent the greater its degree of importance. The life of rural Cape Bretoners revolved around wood and its uses. The ability of Scottish immigrants in particular to adapt themselves to this dominence, coming as they so often did from a treeless hill or island, speaks highly of their ingenuity and resourcefulness.

Cutting wood in the spring could be an agony. It was as if every black fly on the island was attracted to the smell of the fresh sap. There were ways to overcome this. Sometimes the woodsman would cut the tree in the very early hours and then go back after the sun was high and the flies fewer to peel off the bark. Sometimes time pressed too hard to permit this and so the early cutter - before the days of chemical repellants - would cover his face and arms with bear grease. Later axle grease was used. Others tried putting vinegar or lemon juice on themselves. But there were always some bites to contend with and a way a countering the itch was to rub the bite with raw onion.

March is a good season for storing up firewood, cutting softwood for poles, posts and pulp. Pole wood, often black spruce since it is so straight and knot free, was used as slides and rollers for moving heavy loads. The March winds dry out the winter cut firewood logs in the woods, making them easier to haul and the ground is still hard with frost or snow so that horses may be used to haul in the wood. Retired race horses were popular. Not only were they cheap but they quickly adapted to the job of pulling since they had spent their earlier years pulling racing sulkies. Trouble could appear if the leading butt of the log hit a stump while the horse was cantering out of the woods. To avoid injury to the horse or damage to the traces or the whipple tree the chain securring the log was not tied around the log but was secured with “dogs”. These were simply spikes shaped like an E with the centre prong removed. Two or three hammered into the log would secure it. If the butt of the log hit a stump or other obstruction while the horse was pulling it out the “dogs” would jump free and nothing would be damaged. The farmer needed to be careful as well or he could be injured. To avoid being hit by a fast travelling log - particularly when it bounces off an obstruction - long reins were always used. In this way the farmer could control the horse while keeping well clear of the log.

March is also the month for cutting and splitting the wood.

Ogden Nash wrote a satire on the poem “Trees”, and his poem is perhaps a frightening look at the present.

I think that I shall never see
A billboard lovely as a tree.
Perhaps, unless the billboards fall,
I’ll never see a tree at all.

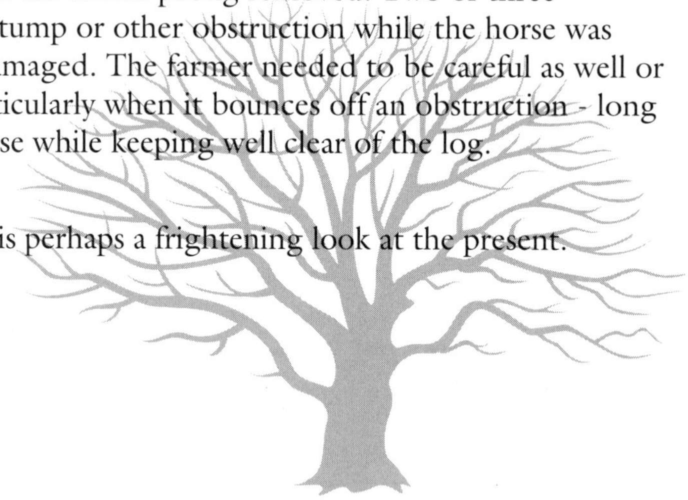

APRIL

How did April get its name? No one knows. But it is the month of new life beginning and so it is associated with the Latin "aperio" to open or display; the month when the Earth opens, the time when the buds of the trees and flowers open. April was considered by the Romans as Venus' month, and Venus was the Greek Aphrodite, the goddess of love, beauty and desire. Wherever she walked flowers sprang up. She was the goddess of pure love as well as the goddess who presided over ordinary love affairs. She ensured conception and consequently procreation.

The Anglo-Saxons called the month *"Estermonath"*, after Eostra, goddess of the dawn, and Easter often comes in April.

The Micmacs called April *"Pnatmuiku's"* - *"the egg laying month"*, while Gaelic-speakers called it *"Ceitein na h-oinsich"* - *"the cuckoo's May"* or *"the fool's May"*. In Europe the cuckoo has long heralded the return of spring. The full moon was the *"Pink Moon"*.

The sun was warm but the wind was chill.
You know how it is with an April day
When the sun is out and the wind is still,
You're one month on in the middle of May.
But if you so much as dare to speak,
A cloud comes over the sunlit arch,
A wind comes off a frozen peak,
And you're two months back in the middle of March.

"Two Tramps in Mudtime" by Robert Frost

April 1 is April Fool's Day, a day to play silly tricks on others. You can be an April fool, a gawk, a cuckoo, a simpleton. In France you can be an April fish, for a young fish is easily caught - a sucker.

But there is a darker, destructive side to April, more like the spring campaigning under Mars. T.S. Eliot describes April as "the cruellest month". This has been true in the Aprils of modern times. The Revolutionary War in the United States began with the battle of Lexington & Concord; the American Civil War began with the firing on Fort Sumter; The Spanish-American War started with an ultimatum to Spain; and war was declared against Germany by the United States in April 1917. In April 1940 in Europe, after months of a phony war, battles began in earnest on the western front against Germany.

We all know the rhyme *"April showers bring May flowers"*. April can be windy as well, and the wind seems to be as welcome as rain. *"When April blows his horn/ 'Tis good for both the hay and corn."*

A major sign of spring is the blossoming of fruit trees. Thousands of people flock to see these blossoms - cherry blossoms in Tokyo and Washington DC, apple blossoms in the Annapolis Valley. The exact season varies with the region, but the response is the same. Other outdoor celebrations include international tulip festivals.

About the woodlands I will go
To see the cherry hung with snow.
"Loveliest of trees" by A.E.Housman

The first apples were planted in Nova Scotia at Port Royal in 1606. However, it wasn't until the end of the 1890's that the apple crop began to gain in importance. Farmers were encouraged to start and extend their orchards. Familiar varieties of the time incuded Gravenstein, Bishop's Pippin, King of Tompkins, R.I. Greening, Ribston Pippin, Northern Spy, Vandevere, and Nonpareil. Many of America's apple trees were planted not only by farmers but also by the legendery Johnny Appleseed.

Apples have always held a position of importance and they have been a symbol of secret knowledge, immortality, eternity and temptations. Magic and secrecy are also connected to apples.

Perhaps the most famous apple came from the tree in the Garden of Eden.

A golden apple was awarded by Paris to Aphrodite, goddess of love, in a beauty contest over the other goddesses. This "apple of discord" as it came to be known, was the cause of the Trojan War as Paris won Helen of Troy, another man's wife.

An apple or an apple branch was the passport to the Celtic otherworld. The legendery King Arthur waited for death with the souls of dead heroes on the Isle of Avalon, the island of apples. The ancient Norsemen believed that apples would magically rejuvenate the gods when they felt they were growing older.

Cut in half, an apple reveals a perfect five-pointed pentagram, another symbol of occult knowledge. Apples were eaten by soothsayers before they made their predictions and prophecies and that great magician Merlin meditated and taught under an apple tree. Mistletoe, another sacred plant, also grows on apple trees.

Another famous apple was the one said to have fallen on Isaac Newton as he sat under an apple tree pondering the laws of Nature.

During World War Two, though, in a popular song a soldier pleads with his girlfriend left back home "Don't sit under the apple tree with anyone else but me".

The fairytale wicked Queen, herself a sorceress, uses a poisoned apple to tempt Snow White who is believed to be dead after she takes a bite.

Apples are healthy and wholesome. Eating one a day is said "to keep the doctor away". Someone especially important to another person is the "apple of his eye". Another famous apple is the "Big Apple", New York City, a place of all kinds of magic and temptation.

In early spring, before winter has left the outside, spring comes inside in the form of major international flower shows: the Chelsea Show in London, The Philadephia Flower Show in Philadelphia, Pennsylvania, the New England Flower Show in Boston, and a spring show in Toronto. Tens of thousands of people come to see the blooms.

Fresh flowers and blossoming trees evoke a widespread response. For both the people viewing them and those people putting on the shows, the live plant materials overwhelm the senses.

Possibly one of the reasons for the popularity of these events is that after winter everyone needs a breath of spring. The colours and the fragrances raise the spirits. For those putting on the shows, the fresh materials pull other responses. Large landscape design arrangements such as a portion of a rain forest or the entire outside facade and garden of a New England country home, complete with the sounds of birds, and flowering trees, grass, and flowers, and the smaller arrangements, interpreting themes, are created with flair, imagination and an intense concentration. The outward spring releases an internal artistic spring.

Another sign of spring is "Fever". *"In the spring a young man's fancy lightly turns to thoughts of love."* (Tennyson). Spring fever hits suddenly. The days are a little longer, the sun a little warmer. And in the northern countries, like our own, we get cabin fever over the winter. Spring is our release. We become lightheaded and foolish.

The skipping ropes, fishing rods, bicycles and baseball bats come from the closets, and we're full of flighty thoughts.

Easter often comes in April. Celebrated on the Sunday after the first full moon following the Spring Equinox, Easter comes between March 21 and April 25. This holiest day in the Christian church celebrates Christ's resurrection. It is connected with older spring celebrations, each festival celebrating new life.

Easter is from the Anglo-Saxon word Oster, meaning rising, and from Eostra, pagan goddess of the dawn, who opened the gates of Valhalla to admit the sun god, and whose radiance flooded the earth in light. Her festival was celebrated at the Spring Equinox. In ancient Rome, festivals were held at the that time for Adonis, god of vegetation and of new life and Christians celebrated the end of the restrictions imposed during Lent.

There is a very old and widespread story that on Easter morning the sun dances with joy in the sky. Pilgrimages were made to the tops of hills to see the sun dance. Pilgrimages are still made to high hills and other outdoor spaces to celebrate with sunrise services.

It was said that if the sun shines on Easter morning it will shine a little every day of the year or that we will have a hot dry summer.

A piece of advice; to keep healthy spread out linen cloths in the garden on Easter Saturday and on Easter morning wash in the dew, rain or snow that has accumulated.

Today we wear new clothes and bonnets for Easter, following the practice of the early Christians who wore new white robes as they were baptized on Easter morning and of the ancients who wore wreaths of leaves on special occasions.

Hares and rabbits are connnected with the spring and with Easter, and, although different animals, over the years they have become interchangeable. The hare and the rabbit are both symbols of fertility and fecundity necessary at this spring season. This symbolism also has a dual nature: fertility and lust, timidity, gentleness and craftiness. The hare is a solitary creature and masculine while the rabbit is gregarious and female. The hare was said to be able to change sexes.

The moon is also connected to death and rebirth, since it appears to die and be reborn each month.

The hare is connected with the moon and with all lunar gods and goddesses. The hare was Eostra's sacred animal and she herself was sometimes called "hare-headed". The deities are either carrying a hare or accompanied by hares.

Moon deities were associated with celestial events. In an Aztec story, the Sun threw a rabbit at the moon to make it darker. The native American Great Hare was able to transform himself. He lived in the moon, and was also known as the hero of the dawn and for recovering the light for his people. Many civilizations believed a hare and not a man lived in the moon. The Buddha, himself a hare in one incarnation, put the hare in the moon.

North American Indians celebrated the Great Hare. In one legend, he appeared as a white light in the night sky, representing the dawn as well as being a sun god. In another extensive legend, the Great Hare, named Manibozho, had a beloved brother who drowned. Grief stricken and angry he covered his face with ashes, retreated into his lodge, and remained there for years. The world became dark and cold, "frostbitten and belly-shrivelled". He was finally enticed out of his lodge. This is very similar to other worldwide legends of the sun's disappearing. (see Winter-December)

Because of their association with witches, hares and rabbits were feared. People believed they caused harm, particularly to dairy cows. Hares were frequently killed since they were believed to be the "familiars" of witches. Shoot the hare with a gun loaded with a crooked silver sixpence and the mark will appear on a human witch.

Hares and rabbits were also bad luck. One seen crossing the road was enough to cancel plans, postpone a visit or a wedding. Miners refused go to work and fishermen returned home.

Despite these fears, parts of the hare and rabbit were used in folk remedies. And a rabbit's foot is still carried as a good luck charm.

Eggs, symbols of creation, new life and fertility are also part of Spring celebrations and both rabbits and hares have, through centuries, delivered coloured eggs at Easter and other Spring celebrations. The egg represents the universe - the shell - the earth and air, the white-symbolizing water, the yolk-fire. Egyptians, Persians, Greeks, Romans, Early Britons and Christians ate coloured eggs during their spring festivals. Jews also eat eggs during Passover, their spring festival.

Eggs are an important symbol and they represent a variety of aspects of life. Eggs laid on Friday cured colic.

An Egghead is considered to be an intellectual. A person can "egg" another person on. "To lay an egg" is a synonym for failure, but this is strange because an egg is the symbol of nature's bounty and certainty.

"Scarce as a hen's teeth". The unborn chick has an egg tooth with which to saw his way out of his shell, but that's promptly absorbed. One walks carefully as if "walking on eggs". An "egg sucker" is one who seeks favor, but telling a person to "suck eggs" is to tell them to go away and not waste your time.

Sucking an egg is actually useful. If you have a sore throat, the egg white clings to the affected parts and stays there like a poultice. The warmth of the yolk as well is good for consumption. Hippocrates, the father of medicine, favored the whites of eggs beaten in three quarts of water as a laxative. Galen, another famous Greek physician, recommended eggs as an excellent diet for the sick, as eggs were easy to digest.

A piece of advice: "Don't put all your eggs in one basket". And remember the fate of Humpty Dumpty - you can't put a broken egg back together.

There are different food traditions at this time. Many Jews have tableware explicitely for this period. Special foods are prepared, including the matzah, an unleavened bread, for the ancient Hebrews only had time to prepare unleavened bread before escaping from their homes and slavery in Egypt.

There are special foods connected with Easter celebrations. Hot cross buns, tiny loaves of bread, spiced and sweetened and with a cross outlined in icing on the top, are special to Good Friday. Buns and breads baked on this day were said never to get moldy. Kept in the home, hanging from a rafter, the buns protected the home against evil and fire, stored corn from mice and clothes from moths. Fishermen carried a bun to protect themselves from shipwrecks and from being lost at sea. In popular medicine, a morsel of bun when grated and mixed with brandy or milk was said to be a cure for diarrehea and other ills.

The custom of eating buns originated in pre-Christian times. In Ancient Greece, a sacred ox was sacrificed to the gods. A representation of its horn was stamped on the small cakes offered to the gods in thanks for the return of spring. Early Egyptians offered their moon goddess cakes marked with horns, symbolizing of the horned ox they had sacrificed. Later the horns became a cross and the Romans ate cakes inscribed with a cross at their sacrifical feasts. At their annual spring festival, the ancient Saxons ate buns inscribed with a cross in honor of their goddess, Eostra. The Chinese, ancient Aztecs and Incas all ate similar cakes to salute their gods.

Eventually specially marked buns were eaten throughout the western world and by the early eighteenth century in London, at the Old Chesea Bun House, as many as one hundred fifty thousand buns were sold on one Good Friday.

Vendors sold them on the street.

One a penny/ Two a penny/ Hot Cross Buns.
If you have no daughters / Give them to your sons.
But if you have none of these merry little elves
Then you may keep them all to yourselves.

Like hot cross buns, lamb has long been associated with spring and with Easter. In Mediterranean countries spring lambs were butchered early because there was little pasture for them. Here in Canada we need an extensive indoor system and early lambing to produce lamb to eat at Easter. This is prohibitive in cost. And because it's unlucky for a shepherd to eat lamb during lambing period, people have come to eat ham instead. However, lamb is a fine meat. It's also been said to be an aphrodisiac.

Jews include lamb in the celebrations of Passover. (See also December)

Shepherds do not sit idly on hillsides, playing a pan flute and gazing at their flocks. In fact, shepherds are very busy, especially at lambing time. The worse the weather - and in the Maritimes we certainly have bad weather in the spring - the more often expectant ewes have to be checked, it doesn't take long for a newborn lamb to chill and die.

Usually the ewes give birth with no problems but a shepherd really needs to be a combination of farmer, midwife and veterinarian. Occasionally though there are problems and help is needed. The shepherd checks throughout the day, last thing at night before going to bed, and, of course, just before dawn - a favorite time for the ewes to lamb.

At the end of the day there are usually "orphan" lambs to tend. If they are chilled or even half frozen having been born and abandonned or mislaid out in the cold, they have to be revived. Often they are brought into the kitchen, dried off and kept warm. Lambs can be revived by dunking them in warm water, then drying them. The lamb can be given a mixture of warm milk and molasses or a shot of rum. They can be kept warm in the oven of the wood range with the door left open, or in a box by the stove. Alternatively they can be placed next to a hot water bottle or Javex bottle filled with hot water and wrapped in an old towel.

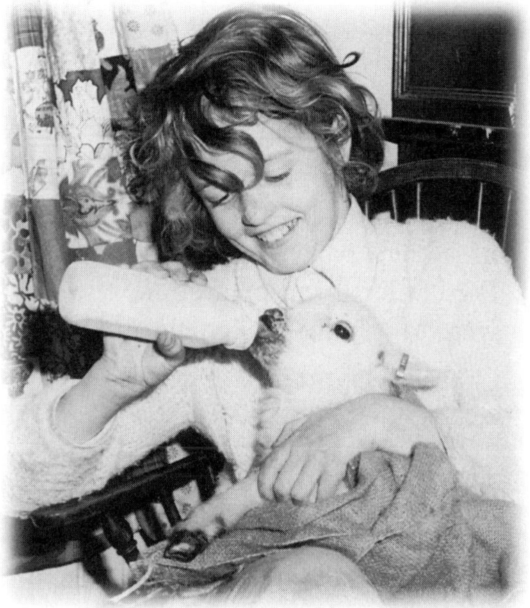

And there are usually other orphan animals or runts to be fussed over. Runt pigs have been known to have been kept warm in a shoe box, lined with wool. Like a lamb he'd be a pet, washed in buttermilk and powdered with talcom powder. Pigs are very loving, and children have been known to cuddle them as they lay on the floor.

Fishing, like lambing, is another sign of spring. But it means more than simply getting out a rod and heading for a secret pond in search of trout.

Fishing has always been fundamental to life in the Maritimes. Hundreds of years ago Basque fishermen netted cod off the coast and Louisbourg Fortress was part of the protection for French fishermen. The economy of the east coast was rooted in the fishing industry and early exports of dried cod to the West Indies resulted in a movement from there to here in sugar, rum and molasses.

Many of the early settlers on Cape Breton came from the highlands and islands of Scotland. They may have been farming crofters who fished, while others were fishermen who farmed. For all, wresting a living from both the land and the sea was part of the cycle of life. Both traditions have continued in this part of the New World.

Fishing was, of course, not confined to new arrivals from Scotland. Micmacs also fished. In mid-March the fish began to spawn and to come up from the sea into certain streams. Swarms of smelts crowded the rivers. They could be scooped by hand they were so plentiful. Sometimes weirs were constructed across a stream and a bag net placed over a small opening in the weir to catch the fish. When the bag net was filled, it was emptied it and the opening covered once more. This fishing was also done at night. Fishermen would carry torches made of birchbark and the fish were attracted to the light and swam close to the canoes where they could be easily speared.

Gasperaux were caught in great numbers on the southwest Margaree River and other rivers. Today they're used mostly for bait, although a few are always a treat salted for the winter and eaten with blue potatoes. Years ago they were used as fertilizer, planted next to the potato rows, not next to the potatoes for they would burn the seed. Gasperaux were caught commercially and salted in barrels right on the river banks.

In the spring Micmacs fished both on the seacoasts for a variety of fish, including shellfish such as oysters and clams, and lobsters, and inland for eels and salmon. They also caught other food abundant on the coasts like seals and walruses. (Today walruses may be extinct. They haven't been seen for a long time, but there are indications that some may have survived.)

When frogs were heard chirping in ponds people knew eels would be coming up. When caught the eels were put in wood ashes, paper or cloth and the slime was cleaned off the outside. The eels were washed, gutted and then flattened and hung up like pieces of cloth to dry.

Eels can be boiled or fried. Just about all the grease gets out if they are baked. Eels are a very rich food; the greasier the better. They keep a person healthy, much like cod liver oil does. Some cooks cut the eels into four inch pieces, bake them in the oven and finish them off by broiling. The skin may be thrown away but some consider it the best part. To make an eel pie: make a bannock-like bread, spread it over the top of prepared eel and bake.

Fishermen say that the best time for fishing varies with the seasons and with the moon. In the cooler months, it's best from noon to about 3 p.m.; in summer from sunset to one hour later. The best day is warm and cloudy, for on a cloudy day the fish feed near the surface.

Fish can sense weather changes and are active three days before a storm. On the actual day of the change they won't bite. A storm is coming if the insects are flying low and the fish are jumping out of the water to catch them. After a heavy rain, the fish may not bite as well, because plenty of food has washed into the lake. Fish are also said to be hard to catch when fresh snow water is in the stream. The best day in a month for fishing is related to the moon's position. Three days before and after the full moon is good, and the two hours before and after the moon is directly overhead.

The next best time is the two hours before and after the moon is straight down on the other side of the earth. Wind direction also has a bearing on the good fishing.

When the wind is in the East,
Then the fishes bite the least;
When the wind is in the West,
Then the fishes bite the best;
When the wind is in the North,
Then the fishes do come forth;
When the wind is in the South,
It blows the bait in the fish's mouth.
Anonymous.

The fishing season begins, in many Maritime coastal communities, with the Blessing of the Fleet. The fishing boats of an area gather at one port. Each boat is decorated with flags and streamers and crowds of people stand along the quayside to participate in the occasion. A local priest blesses the fleet and prays for a safe and successful season.

Meanwhile, back on the farm, there is a lighter side to life. Today we can buy everything we need or want in stores. But for many living in rural areas that wasn't as easy as it is now. And people made do with what they had. Even for something as simple as chewing gum. Many people headed for a nearby spruce tree. Little round lumbs of spruce sap congealed on the exterior of the bark would be peeled off and used as a gum for chewing.

Louisbourg Fortress had a reputation for brewing spruce beer. First the French troops were issued molasses to make the beer and civilians stationed there made the brew once the reserves of other liquors had run out. When the British took over the fort, they quickly acquired the art in the belief, real or contrived, that the water there was bad for health. The British used a ratio of six quarts of molasses to a barrel of water, similar to the Newfoundlanders' recipe, while the French used a ratio of four quarts of molasses to the barrel of water. Tender strips of spruce or pine were boiled for three hours then the liquid was strained into a wooden cask and the molasses added.

At this time sap is rising in the trees and it easier to peel off the bark. In the more distant past the bark was removed so that, when the wood was used for buildings insects would not nest underneath the bark. More recently bark was peeled off short lengths of pulp wood - most softwoods - which is usually sold for export to Europe. Short pulp was generally cut in four foot or three foot six inch lengths. Before the sap rose the farmer used the short blade of a brush scythe and wrapped rags around each end to act as handles. Then, resting the log on a "saw-horse" for support he pulled the blade towards himself, drawing off the bark - so it's called "draw shaving". Once the sap had started to rise all he needed do was draw off one sliver of bark. Then he pushed the blade of a small axe, or similar implement, under the remaining bark and rotated the log. The bark then peeled off. Frequently the farmer cut and limbed full lengths of spruce in the woods and dragged or "twitched" the logs out to the roadside with a horse. The log was cut into the required lengths and peeled at the roadside.

It was said that wood cut in May was useless for house framing and finishing, but it had the toughness and rubberlike quality needed for the handles of implements. The right kind of wood gives a good "feel" to a hammer handle. Yellow birch was pliable enough to cut and be used to make brooms.

At this time of year the roads and their poor condition, still affect everyone. Tarmac or dirt, they deteriorate rapidly as the frost leaves the ground, and heavy vehicles are still banned on many. The public is given some sort of warning that the road conditions are poor. As bad as bumps and heaving roads - perhaps worse - are the potholes. Dirt roads turn into quagmires and many travellers have been stranded.

At first there were no roads or bridges. Everything that was needed was far from the settler, except (as one Middle River man remembered) *"the wood; that was at the door, and too near the house when trees were felled. We had no bridges then, just trees* (over the river), *and when the river was high, the water would be over them. Five were drowned because of lack of bridges."*

Roads remained poor for a long time - even into the 1920's. In 1930 there was some construction and reconstruction. It wasn't until the winter of 1949-50 that roads in Victoria County were improved enough to be made passable year-round. Snowploughs could now be used and the doctor, along with other drivers, could now use his car to get around the countryside instead of his horse and sleigh.

Men were always available for roadwork since the practice was to give the first chance for work to residents along the stretch of road being repaired. Nowadays this principle appears to be still followed with the first hired for clearing brush which obstructs vision along the roadside being given to the immediate householders who need the work.

Fishing villages were isolated with very little communication between them except by water. Many people living far away from some of those isolated communities had odd ideas about them (much like Americans have about Canada today). People in Sydney thought that Down North there were icebergs and polar bears.

Road conditions made spring traveling difficult. Horses had an easier time in the other seasons. Horses were an important part of the farm family, doing both field and hauling work. Many farms had five or six of them, each with its particular chores, one good driving horse and the rest work horses. In winter, each had its distinct bell, so one could hear lots of jingling as the sleighs rushed along. The 1887 catalogue for an Agricultural and Industrial Exhibition at Mabou, a time when Inverness county led the province in agricultural produce, lists many categories and prizes for horses. For example, first prize for a stallion to breed horses for agricutural purposes was ten dollars, a great amount of money at that time. There were also categories for breeding for agricultural and draft purposes, for trotting, carriage or road horse. Today's categories reflect the pleasure aspect of raising horses, with classes for English and Western pleasure riding horses, barrel racing as well as classes for heavy horses.

Spring cleaning is another tradition of the season. It's time for going through the house room by room, cleaning every corner, every cupboard, from attic to cellar. Doors and windows are thrown open to let in fresh air. An ancient tradition, it's the time to sweep out the old. In the distant past cleanliness was used as a weapon and witches and evil spirits were swept out along with the winter's dust. A vestige of this superstition remained until recently as some people called "blue devils" the lint and dust that shakes free from long winter underwear. Even fires in stoves and fireplaces were allowed to go out. A fresh start is made to the year.

Heavy clothing is put away. Winter items like blankets are washed, hung to dry on clotheslines, porch rails, over shrubbery. In the days before indoor plumbing and running water, it was easier to haul the wash tubs and washboard outside, to make a fire and fill up a big boiler with water. Heavy bulky clothes could be rinsed in the brook and dried on the grass, turning them over to dry on all sides. They could be left out for a couple of nights. The longer they were left, the whiter they would get.

It wasn't just the house that got off to a fresh start. People did as well.

Spring was the season for tonics which help to clean the blood and to get the body going for a new busy season. Sulphur and molasses was the best known tonic. Maple sap or a tea made from the inner bark of the maple tree was drunk by both Indians and early settlers as a blood purifier. Garlic eaten with butter was sometimes recommended. A tea made from the leaves of the mayflower was popular. It was also helpful in treating kidney and bladder disorders, stomachaches, headaches, and sore throats.(The roots were a good luck charm for winning games.)

Teas made of burdock or of the inner bark of wild cherry trees or of wild strawberries later in the season were good but some people thought that dandelion was best of all. To make; boil dandelions and strain. To the juice add one half teaspoon yeast and one quarter cup of sugar. Drink as a beverage by the glassful. As a tonic it's particularly good for elderly people. Dandelion greens were as good as iron pills. Three feeds in the spring got you going.

Dandelions are nutritious, with vitamin A, thiamin, ribofalavin, vitamin C, calcium, sodium and potassium. The young roots, dug before the last frost of spring, are good as a cooked vegetable. The greens are eaten before the flowers bloom. Eaten raw or cooked they taste like spinach. They have also been considered an aphrodisiac.

To help "balance the body" a tonic that cont inues to be useful to take every day of the year is two teaspoons of honey with two teaspoons of apple cider vinegar to a glass of water.

MAY

May is named after Maia, a Roman goddess of growth and increase, to whom sacrifices were made on the first day of this month. Maia was the eldest and most beautiful of the "sisters", the group of stars in the Pleiades. She was seduced by Zeus and gave birth to Hermes, the messenger of the gods. May has been described as a beautiful maiden, clothed in sunshine, and scattering flowers on the earth while she dances to the music of birds and brooks.

Other names include the Anglo-Saxon *"Tri-Milchi"*, for the improved condition of the cattle who were now able to give milk three times a day; the Gaelic word was *"Mios bochuin"* - *"the month of swelling"*; the Celtic word was *"Winnemanoth"* - *"Joy Month"*; and the Micmacs called the month *"Tqoljewiku's"* - *"the time of frog croaking"*. The full moon in that month has been called *"the Flower Moon"*.

Now is the month of Maying, When merry lads are playing.
Fa la la la la la la la la la.
Each with his bonny lass, A-dancing on the grass.
Fa la la, la la, Fa la la la la la.
The spring, clad all in gladness, Doth laugh at winter's sadness.
Fa la la la la la la la la la.

Now is the Month of Maying by Thomas Morley

May Day. The first of May is a special day. You can ensure a good complexion by going out in the fields, just as the sun rises, and washing your face in the dew.

It is a day that has been celebrated through the ages. Flora, goddess of flowers and blooming vegetation, had her festival on May Day and it was celebrated with a feast of flowers rather than with sacrifices. In England it was common for groups of young people to go to the woods at the midnight heralding the first of May. They would go with music, gather branches of pink and white hawthorn flowers, and carry them home at sunrise. Queen Elizabeth I said, *"of 100 maidens going to the wood overnight, there are scarcely the third part of them returned home again undefiled."*

The most conspicuous feature of these celebrations was the Maytree or Maypole. A tall tree was cut down and the branches lopped off, except a few at the top. Carried to the village it was set up and decorated. It was believed to have powers of fertility over both humans and livestock. At first people danced around the tree, the tree later became a pole. Each person held the end of a long streamer that had been fastened to the top of the Maypole and everyone then circled around the pole crisscrossing the ribbons. This wove the ribbons together and at the end of the dance they covered the whole Maypole.

"The month of May was come, when every heart beginneth to blosssom, and to bring forth fruit; for like as herbs and trees bring forth fruit and flourish in May, in likewise every lusty heart that is in any manner a lover, springeth and flourish in lusty deeds. For it giveth unto all lovers courage, that lusty month of May." (*"Le Morte d'Arthur"* by Sir Thomas Malory)

A modern addition to May Day is the May basket, a little basket made of paper and filled with flowers and hung on a friend's doorknob.

May Day acquired additional meanings. The labour movement in Europe and the United States celebrated the first of May as a labor day, a time to seek better working conditions.

May Day is an important political day for the Communists so, in response, in the United States May Day is Loyalty Day, and Labour Day was moved to September.

May Day is also the international distress call, but it has nothing to do with spring. It's from the French "m'aidez", "help me".

No one wants thunder in May. It frightens summer away and presages a poor summer and harvest.

"Though April Showers may come your way, They bring the flowers that bloom in May", most importantly our Nova Scotia flower, the Mayflower. They also bring the tulips, which bloom after the other spring bulbs: crocus, grape hyacinths, snowdrops, hyacinths and daffodils.

Fresh wild greens begin to grow, and are particularly welcomed after a winter's diet. In the "good old days" they were an important part of our food since there were no supermarkets for a year-round supply of fresh greens. Fiddleheads, ferns with the fronds still curled, were prized as was wood sorrel with its shamrock shaped leaves, found in mossy banks in the woods. Lamb's quarters, a common weed found in waste places and cultivated fields, flowers throughout the summer and is considered one of the best wild greens. The leaves of all of these wild plants are boiled and served with butter and seasoning. Most taste much like spinach and are rich in minerals.

The month is unlucky for kittens, which are said to become melancholic, and it's also an unlucky month for marriages, perhaps lending to the popularity of June as a good time.

But a warning. Don't take off your longjohns too early in May or you'll come down with a spring cold.

"Shear your sheep in May, you'll shear them away." The weather is too unpredictable for shorn sheep, who will catch cold and die. Even if they don't die, their milk will dry up and their lambs will.

A sign of spring on Cape Breton is "the Burning of the Grass". Every year it is as though a switch were flipped. This is rationalized as encouraging the new growth of grass, but it is as if some pyromania grips the people to the anguish of local fire departments. What is this craze? Does it really just mean that people want to get rid of unsightly, long dry grass? Or can it be that it has a different meaning. Perhaps we are answering an unconscious urge, one that connects us back through time to the ancient days of our ancestors.

All over Europe people used to make great bonfires on certain days of the year. The spring fires were usually close to the beginning of May. This day was known to the ancient Celts as Beltane Day. It marked the turning point in the year, important with new vegetation and the cattle were put out to pasture. It marked summer's beginning. The god of the herd and the harvest was invoked to ensure prolific births and crops. The more bonfires that could be seen flaring in the darkness, the more fruitful the year was expected to be.

People danced around fires and leapt over glowing embers. The higher the leaps, the better the crops. Torches were lit from the bonfires and carried through the orchards and fields and gardens, wherever fruit trees were, passing the burning torch under the branches of every tree to make them fruitful.

Fires destroyed sickness. Cattle and sheep and people were sent over the dying embers or around or between the fires and so were purified. The fires in the houses that had been extinguished were lit again with "new fire" from these special bonfires. Fires also purified the area of witches, who were believed to be responsible for all sickness, infertility and all other misfortunes. Even the ashes from the fires were important as they were believed to have healing properties.

Other fires, wheels of burning straw which were rolled down hills, were sun charms, to ensure a steady supply of sunshine through the growing season.

May was the time for mending fences and for repairing, whitewashing and building barns and other outhouses, the name given any building away from the main house.

Land was cleared, and that meant still more bonfires. Today farmers often put several rubber tires into the heaps of brush. When they burn, and they do with an intense heat, they ensure that the green wood will catch and keep burning.

The early settlers used the ash of the burned trash to advantage. First, the trash to be burned was piled around the stumps of trees to make their removal easier. After the fires were out and the ashes had cooled, potatoes were planted and the natural potash helped ensure a good crop of new potatoes.

Dynamite was also used to remove stubborn stumps and also to fragment particularly large rocks.

Victoria Day weekend was, and still is, the traditional time for planting potato seed. First it had to be cut. Whole potatoes could be used but these early farmers had to be even more economical than they are today. Many farmers had kept over winter their greened potatoes (those which had been touched by sunlight while growing, had a sharp taste and were possibly slightly poisonous) to be used for seed. Others put their smaller potatoes to one side. But all potatoes designated for seed and with more than three eyes showing were, come the spring, cut for seed. Seed pieces were wedge-shaped and had two or three eyes each so that it was often possible to get two or even three pieces of good seed from one potato.

Another sign of spring was the arrival of the peddlars. In the early part of this century merchandise was sold throughout the rural areas by peddlars, usually new immigrants to Canada. Lebanese and Jews from eastern Europe dominated this trade. They started with packs on their backs. Dave Epstein came to Cape Breton in the early 1900's from Russian Poland when he was fifteen. Relatives here already helped get him started. *"They made me a pack and sent me to the country peddling. There were all kinds of dry goods - little notions, towels, soap, hairpins, and all that, mostly for the ladies: wrappers, dresses and petticoats and all kinds of stuff. By the time they made up the pack, it was 125 pounds"*, recalled Dave Epsein in "Cape Breton's Magazine". On his first trip he travelled north to Ingonish on the boat the "Aspy" where he was met by a relative who had peddled in Victoria County the previous year and who now owned a horse to help him. Over the next seven months Dave Epstein, like many others, travelled, covering the same route two or three times, taking a boat to Neil's Harbour, then walking to Dingwall and Sugarloaf and back. He spoke no English but was made welcome, staying overnight at various homes, where he paid by barter - leaving a towel or a bar of soap.

About the same time two Lebanese sisters peddled between North Sydney and Mulgrave. Stories told in the Ballah household are of the family's intentions to go into business and peddling was the only way they could get a start. Carrying two heavy valises filled with goods, the sisters headed down the road. After their first day of peddling they were very tired and hungry and were attracted to the smell of cooking food at a farmhouse. They were invited in for a meal. On seeing the table set for supper one of the exhausted women broke down and sobbed. They could not speak English at first but, like the other peddlers, they were welcomed throughout the countryside. Another story tells of an incident with a farmer who gave the sisters a lift in his wagon. When he made amorous advances, they beat him up and left him by the side of the road.

Later it was the Raleigh or Watkins representative who came around selling spices and cleaning items. His arrival was a break from farm routine and was welcomed every spring.

Peddlars weren't the only ones walking. People thought nothing of walking long distances: two miles to the local store and two miles back home, three miles to a neighbour's house for a visit, and sometimes up to five or six miles to a dance.

People walked over the mountains from New Campbellton to St.Anns for the Reverend Norman MacLeod's church services. Others walked or came by horse and buggy or by boat from nearby communities and from as far away as Whycocomagh, a trip that would take about fifty minutes by car today.

May 24 - Victoria Day, originally known as Empire Day, celebrates the birthday of Queen Victoria. The holiday weekend is considered to be the first weekend of summer.

Summer

June/ July/ August

In the good old summertime, in the good old summertime
Strolling thro' the shady lanes, With your baby mine;
You hold her hand and she holds yours, And that's a very good sign
That she's your tootsey wootsey in the good old summertime.
"In the Good Old Summertime" by Ren Shields

Shall I compare thee to a summer's day?
Thou art more lovely and more temperate...
by William Shakespeare

JUNE

June is named after the Roman goddess Juno, queen of the gods and ruler of the high point of the year, the time of maximum light and minimum darkness, goddess of the moon, of women and of childbirth. June is favored for marriages.

In Gaelic the month of June was *"An t'Og mhios"* - *"the young month"*; in Anglo-Saxon it was *"Litha"* - *"the month of the Midsummer moon"*; in Micmac it was *"Saqatpewiku's"* - *"nature unfolding"*. The full moon of June has been known as the *"Fallow Moon", the "Hot"* or *"Strawberry Moon"*.

By mid-month we are "knee-deep in June" said the poet James Whitcomb Reily; the senses are piqued and quickened by the smells, sounds and subtle presences of early summer.

And what is so rare as a day in June?
Then, if ever, come perfect days.
"The Vision of Sir Launfal" by James Russell Lowell

A thing of beauty is a joy forever;
Its loveliness increases; it will never
Pass into nothingness; but still will keep
A bower quiet for us, and a sleep
Full of sweet dreams, and health, and quiet breathing.
Therefore, on every morrow, are we wreathing
A flowery band to bind us to the earth.
"Endymion" by John Keats

As they sing in Rogers and Hammerstein's "Carousel", *"June is bustin' out all over".*

People are bustin' out all over as well; children will soon be out of school and, with the start of summer vacations, people all over Canada are heading for country cottages. The urge to return to the country overtakes everyone.

The weather of June dramatically changes and affects all life. It used to be said, if you heard blue birds chirping (complaining) "I want my tea", it would rain within a day or two. An early adage was *"June damp and warm/ Doth the farmer no harm."*

Summer is unofficially here when we can pick dandelions to make wine.

Angelica, the plant with a tall thick stem, looking much like an umbrella, grows wild along the shores and ditches. Now common along our roadsides it was originally brought here by the French garrison stationed at Louisbourg and it is said that today it is only extensively found in North America on Cape Breton and around New Orleans, both places where French troops were stationed. Although now a weed, it was once a prized herb, grown deliberately in gardens for both culinary and medicinal purposes.

The whole angelica plant is sweetly aromatic with the odor resembling that of licorice. The tender leaves, stalks and stems can be boiled or roasted like potatoes or eaten raw in salads, and the bigger leaves are wrapped around fish to keep the flies off.

Angelica stewed with rhubarb complements the flavour and reduces the acid taste, so that less sugar is needed.

Candied angelica makes a prized cake or pastry decoration, being deep green in colour. It can also be made into a mildly flavoured chewy candy by adding a little gelatine to the sugar pan during candying. Commercially, angelica seeds help flavour gin, and the dried roots are ingredients of brandy, vermouth, Benedictine and Chartreuse.

Known as "the herb of the Holy Ghost", angelica was known for its medicinal uses in combating the plague, aiding digestion and elimination, as an aid against snake bites and rabies, and tremblings of the heart.

Baa baa, black sheep,
Have you any wool?
Yes sir, yes sir
Three bags full.

That is a lot of wool from one sheep. Nevertheless, the rhyme has been around for centuries. Farmers here tried to keep a black sheep or two just for their wool. They liked the colour range and found the wool good for making socks

possibly because black or grey toned socks don't show the dirt as quickly. In olden times black wool was considered useful in healing. It could be wrapped around an injured limb or put over a congested chest.

With the arrival of more predictable fine weather, it's time for shearing. Even when the price of wool is down, the sheep still have to be shorn. Some farmers did it themselves, others used the services of a travelling shearer.

There are different types of wool. Today on Cape Bretona a popular breed is the North Country Cheviot or close crosses. Having been bred for the raw wet hills between Scotland and England the wool coats of these sheep are compact and readily shed the cold rains. The long wooled Scottish Blackface sheep, also found in Nova Scotia has a more open and longer fleece, and an undercoat of finer wool, that sheds the rain. Not all breeds are so hardy. The world famous Scottish tweeds owe their reputation to the wool of the Cheviot, finer than that of the Blackface. However, there are two basic types of sheep; those bred to produce wool - and they generally thrive in the hot dry climate of places like Australia - and those bred to produce meat. They do best in climates like our own, or Scotland, or for the fatter breeds, the gentler fields of Ontario. Said a poet, *"The mountain sheep are sweeter but the valley sheep are fatter. We therefore deemed it meeter to carry off the latter."*

The sheep of Cape Breton, mountain sheep, sweeter sheep, have been highly regarded, but this may be more a result of the type of management than consideration of breed. Cape Breton sheep, often sent off to fend for themselves after shearing and left out ranging the field and woods until the snow flies, have had a wide foraging range and an almost limitless choice of fodder - from wild berries to clovers, grasses and even some browsing. This has produced mothers with an abundance of milk and very high quality lambs raised on that milk. Some sheep have grazed along the shoreline and lambs raised by mothers that have eaten the fronds of seaweed along the shore by Gabarus know few equals.

This superiority of Cape Breton lamb has been widely recognised. As early as 1734 records indicate that a settler, Julian Fizel, was raising sheep at Framboise and Forchu for consumption by the soldiers at Louisbourg. The growth of this type of livestock raising was slow and by the end of the eighteenth century there were barely six hundred sheep here, mainly at Isle Madame, Cheticamp, Port Hood and Louisbourg. However, even then some were being exported to Newfoundland. By 1801 the numbers had grown to over two thousand six hundred although at this time the human population was just over two thousand five hundred. Then came the great leap forward and eighty years later, in 1881, numbers had reached one hundred and seven thousand. This was not because there were big sheep farms here but because there were a lot a small farms, each possibly with a few dozen or so head. Inverness County had the greatest numbers.

The industrialization of the economy brought the decline of the sheep industry. Farmers from all across the island left the fields for the cash wages of the steel plant or the mines. After a few years spruce was growing again on fields so laboriously cleared and many, however they may have been disillusioned by the promises of the city, felt that there was no going back. By 1901 numbers of sheep had slipped to eighty seven thousand, by 1951 to forty three thousand and by 1961 to six thousand. There was a revival with an importation organized by the Cape Breton Development Corporation in 1975 but today numbers are close to what they were twenty years ago - with one difference; the importation of top quality breeding stock has resulted in higher quality and North Country Cheviots from Cape Breton are among the best on the continent.

This recent decline in numbers, however, has been to a large extent the consequence of the coyote. This predator has meant that a great many farmers would have to bring their flocks in to the barn at night, limiting their ability to carry large numbers. The coyote also threatened the community pastures at Mabou and Mira which for some years felt unable to accept sheep because of the risk. There was a bitter humour to a slogan of the Canadian Sheep Producers' Association, "Eat Canadian Lamb, 10,000 coyotes can't be wrong." Despite all the predations those farmers who have continued to raise sheep during these difficult years have found a ready market for choice lamb and gourmets quickly recognize the difference in quality between the home grown product and the import from New Zealand or Australia.

Shearing sheep is an annual chore, generally done with reluctance. Some, impatient to finish the job, start too early and then the sheep, feeling the cold, do not produce enough milk to thoroughly satisfy their lambs. Generally it is best to wait. Enough wool was kept for the family's use and the rest sent off to the mill. (See also September)

Raw wool was washed outside and let dry. Further pieces of wool soiled with dirt or manure were taken out. Then the wool was carded. The cards were rectangular wooden paddles with handles and wires on one side of the paddle. The wool was put between the wire sides and gently combed (carded), pulling the wool further apart - the right handed card pulling in one direction and the left handed card in the other direction - and made into a rolag, a long thin roll of wool. These rolags were later spun, drawn out and twisted into a continuous thread of yarn.

The bigger the sheep's grazing range, the further the fences, the more important the sheep dog. There are all sorts of sheep dogs. There are German Shepherds and Afghans. The Lassie type collie has for many years been bred for show and it may be that its sheep handling instincts have become lost or at least submerged. Among professional sheep herders the popular dog is the Border Collie. Small, fast, obedient and exceptionally intelligent, the Border Collie at work is amazing. With a distinctive series of whistles and hand motions the shepherd will have his dog circling sheep on some distant hill, gather them into a group and carefully, while avoiding panic, drive the flock to wherever the shepherd wants it. Some believe the the dog loves the sheep. This is far from the truth. It is discipline, training and respect for his master's wishes that makes the Border Collie king - or queen - of sheep-herding dogs. Watch the eyes of a dog at work; sometimes a stubborn ram will stand up to the dog, stamping its hoof in the face of the approaching collie. Then the dog drops flat and out-stares the ram. If the ram still holds his ground then the collie will make a short, sharp rush in its direction. If the ram still faces up to the collie, then he will make a snap at the ram's face. No ram will stand up to this psychological pressure for long and, if he has been too stubborn, the collie may even make a move to snap at his fleeing hoof. It seems that the instinct of the Border Collie is to circle and then chase sheep - and chasing sheep is the ultimate sin of a good dog. But the collie has been trained to curb this instinct and do precisely what his shepherd demands of him.

Dogs, unless they are trained sheep dogs, are a menace for the sheep farmer. A flock of sheep that has been chased by a dog suffers from it. At the very least they are over excited and become more difficult to manage. They may also, in their fright, smash into fences and injure themselves, and if they have been bred they may well suffer from spontaneous abortion, thus destroying for at least a year, their potential for revenue. Many dogs will, of course, not confine their activities to running the sheep. They kill or maim as well, tearing at the flanks of the older sheep and biting the life from the lambs.

The sheep industry is built on thousands of years of experience. As a result many customs and expressions whose meaning are lost in the mists of antiquity have come down to us.

A system of counting sheep is necessary. Originally these rhymes probably were also used to pick people out for sacrifice. They were used to rapidly count animals as they passed through a narrow gate. *"One, two, three,"* etc" becomes *" Yan, tan, tethera, nethera, pimp, sethera, lethera, hovera, devera, dick."* Then you *"yan a dick, tan a dick"* and so on, the shepherds notching the twenties on their sticks incredibly swiftly as the sheep rush past.

This method is a survival from the past ascribed variously to the Celts, the Romans, the Welsh, the Greeks, the Romanies (gypsies) and even possibly to the Basques. There are considerable local variations to the counting rhymes. One of these variations was to add onto the old nursery rhyme *"This litttle pig went to market and this is the way to count the pigs - yan, tan, tehera, etc."*

Today these rhymes survive as children's counting rhymes to pick people for teams or as rhymes for skipping rope and other games.

Eenie, meenie, miney mo
Crack a fenney, finey fo
Ommanuga, poppatuga,
Rick, stick, dan, do.

Inty, minty, dibity fig
Dilah, dalah, dominig
Ikah, pikah, dominika
Elika, belika, boo
Out goes you.

Eenie, meenie, miney mo
Catch a rabbit by the toe
If he hollars let him go
Eenie, meenie, miney, mo
Out goes you.

June 9 - St. Columba's Day was considered the luckiest day of the year in Highland Scotland, especially if it fell on a Thursday. St. Columba is associated with the start of certain activities at this time of year. He was an Irish monk in the sixth century who journeyed to the Scottish Highlands to spread the word of God and was given the island of Iona on which to establish a monastery. His name is given to a Cape Breton church in our community of Iona. On his day it was proclaimed:

Day of Colum Cille the beloved
Day to put the loom to use
Day to put sheep to pasture
Day to put the coracle on the sea
Day to bear, day to die
Day to make prayer efficacious
Day of my beloved, the Thursday.
"Carmina Gadelica"

Summer Solstice, June 2l, the day the sun shines the longest, was believed to be one of the most powerful days of the year. At Stonehenge in England there is the most dramatic dawn, for on this day, from the centre of the circle of megalithic stones, the sun rises exactly at the heelstone arch.

The sun has always been important in our lives, and it was even more so in ancient times. The sun appearing on time and as predicted made this day, at a time before calenders, powerful and mysterious. Midsummer Day, falling three days later, was part of the same celebration of the sun, and was greeted with bonfires and torchlight parades.

Evening was important because, in ancient times, the day was counted as starting not at midnight but at sunset of the day before. Midsummer Eve was dangerous and frightening. Some believed the soul could temporarily leave the body and wander. Terrified that this would happen, people would stay awake to keep vigil. This possibility of the soul wandering matched beliefs at Halloween, another dangerous day. For though the souls of the living could wander at Midsummer's Eve, at Halloween it was the souls of the dead. Some people were not frightened. They welcomed the opportunity to cavort with strange souls and to do this they sought to induce invisibility by eating the seeds of a fern.

The early Christians designated June 24, Midsummer's Day, to be St. John the Baptist's Day. John the Baptist, the herald and precursor of Christ, was called by Christ "a burning and a shining light". This is a Christian expression of the strength, power and mystery of the sun at this time of year. The other major sun celebration was six months later at the Winter Solstice and at Christmas.

St. Jean the Baptist Day, or Jean Baptiste Day, was brought to Canada by French settlers who celebrated with parades, bonfires, carnivals and street dances, very much like the earlier customs of lighting bonfires to celebrate the sun and staying awake keeping civic vigil.

Our England is a garden that is full of stately views,
Of borders, beds and shrubberies and lawns and avenues,
With statues on the terraces and peacocks strutting by;
But the Glory of the Garden lies in more than meets the eye.

And some can pot begonias and some can bud a rose,
And some are hardly fit to trust with anything that grows;
But they can roll and trim the lawns and sift the sand and loam,
For the Glory of the Garden occupieth all who come.

Our England is a garden, and such gardens are not made
By singing: - "Oh, how beautiful!" and sitting in the shade,
While better men than we go out and start their working lives
At grubbing weeds from gravel-paths with broken dinner knives.

There's not a pair of legs so thin, there's not a head so thick,
There's not a hand so weak and white, nor yet a heart so sick,
But it can't find some needful job that's crying to be done,
For the Glory of the Garden glorifieth everyone.

Then seek your job with thankfulness and work till further orders
If it's only netting strawberries or killing slugs on borders;
And when your back stops aching and your hands begin to harden,
You will find yourself a partner in the Glory of the Garden.

Oh, Adam was a gardener, and God who made him sees
That half a proper gardener's work is done upon his knees,
So when your work is finished, you can wash your hands and pray
For the Glory of the Garden, that it may not pass away!
And the Glory of the Garden it shall never pass away.

"The Glory of the Garden" by Rudyard Kipling

Beginning with the Garden of Eden, and continuing in a variety of forms throughout the ages, gardens have been more than simply places to grow vegetables and flowers. A personal relationship develops between the gardener and nature. Gardens are individual expressions. They can be decorative or functional or both, for the garden feeds us mentally and spiritually as well as physically.

We cannot garden without a direct involvement, an active relationship with the soil and plants. Our physical bodies are fed by the food we grow. Our work keeps us physicaly active and stimulates all the senses.

Gardens are places where our minds relax, where both mental and physical stress are reduced, and where we can meditate and shut out the busy world around us. In the garden we find that we can control a small part of the world which too often seems overwhelming.

Gardens also feed our spiritual bodies, our souls, and by tying us to nature, create something bigger than ourselves.

Today many people garden for recreation. By the mid 1990's, gardening had become the top hobby in North America. Some large corporations are providing gardening space for their employees. Occupational and physio-therapists have long recognised the theraputic value of gardening. As Rudyard Kipling has written in the above poem, *"There's not a pair of legs so thin, there's not a head so thick,/ There's not a hand so weak and white, nor yet a heart so sick,/ But it can't find some needful job that's crying to be done."*

Gardens have always been places of refuge and privacy. They separated the forests and wilderness from the places brought under cultivation; they shut out wild animals. Today the wilderness has been replaced by a jungle of concrete, and gardens remain a retreat from the outside world.

Long ago, the English started to enclose their gardens with thorn hedges, ditches, banks of earth, fencing and walls, through which the only entrance was a locked door or gate. In parts of Newfoundland today, the yards and houses are fenced off while the sheep, wild ponies and occasional cow roam the rest of the area.

In the Middle Ages most people in England had a yard or garden attached to their houses. One difference between the cottage and big well-to-do gardens was that in cottage gardens the fruit trees, vegetables, herbs and flowers all grew together, whereas larger gardens were sectioned off, so that the vegetable patch was surrounded by the more carefuly arranged flower and herb garden.

Castles had gardens. Churches had gardens. Companies and guilds had gardens.

By the late 1400's the population had risen so much that there wasn't room for everyone to have a garden behind his house, and the garden plots were then arranged around the edges of the towns. Our modern allotment gardens, mostly started during the Second World War to provide additional food for families on rations, have a medieval heritage.

People then depended on their gardens. They were an economic necessity. The medieval poet, Geoffrey Chaucer, when he wanted to portray someone completely destitute wrote, *"She did not even have a vegetable garden. She was reduced to gathering her vegetables from the wilds and waysides and other people's gardens"*.

Today, ornaments and statues in gardens are simply decorations. But originally they were there to protect the garden from evil spirits.

Fashionable gardeners in Europe built banks of earth against the walls surrounding their gardens. Then they faced them with stone or brick, and planted the top with sweet smelling herbs. They put turf seats in recesses cut into the walls, where the women, for whom these gardens were a refuge and a delight, could sit in peace, doing needlework or playing with their pets, talking with friends or making flower garlands.

In the middle of the nineteenth century, one patronizing man wrote of women and gardening. A corner of the estate garden was set aside, he said, for her to control. It was a place where she could do no mischief, where she could pursue her own little fancies (such highly unconventional activities as raising wildflowers or leaving shrubs to grow).

There is satisfaction in growing things and a value that has no monetary price. According to an ancient Chinese proverb, *"He who plants a garden plants happiness."* As an 1855 handbook on gardening comments, *"Is not a nosegay from one's own beds and borders more valued than twenty times the quantity would be derived from another source?"*

There are various types and sizes of gardens. Symetrical gardens, for example, are detailed and elaborate patterns, created by using mirror images and the textures and shades of green to help form the pattern. One example of this type of garden is the Engineer's garden at the Fortress of Louisbourg. Other gardens are less formal. As industrialization progressed, the English sought to make their gardens less formal and more natural.

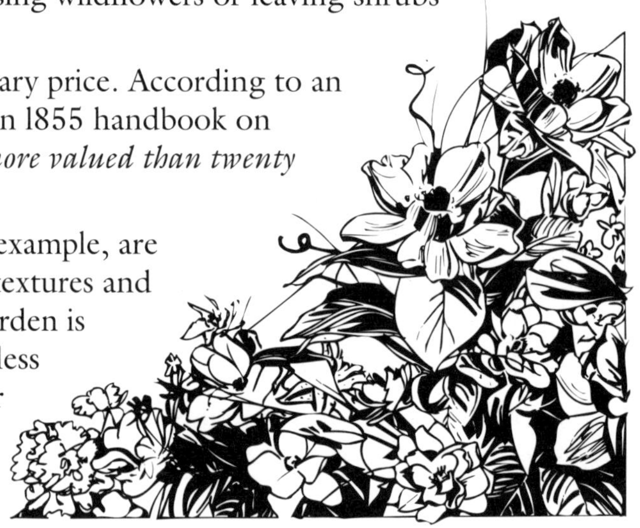

Many people throughout the centuries have believed in planting by the moon. It was suggested that crops that produce above ground should be planted during the waxing of the moon, as it increased in size and light. And that crops producing below ground be planted as the moon waned, as it decreased.

Sometimes an egg was planted along with the seeds to inspire the seeds to "hatch" a good crop. Iron nails were planted with apple trees to give the apple flesh its flavourful reddish streaks. Seaweed or a fish planted by each hill of corn seeds was to help ensure productivity. Other gardening advice comes from Prince Charles who suggests, *"To get the best results you must talk to your vegetables."*

In nature plants seldom grow in pure stands. They like to grow in mixtures which tend to be healthier than single crops. Mixed plantings attract a variety of insects which appear at different times and provide a steady supply of food for insect predators.

The growing of unrelated plants next to each other for the benefit of both has been used with varying success. A comfort zone is created where plants are better able to resist insects and diseases.

Some plants are able to attract or repel insects. Eggplants and beans attract the Colorado potato beetle away from the potato. But the natural chemical resistance of plants to pests can be made ineffective by the use of weed killers and insecticides. Toxic chemicals do more than kill insects or weeds. They destroy the subtle pattern of chemical interactions that plants generate for their own protection. Not every bug is a bad bug, and not every good bug is a dead bug

More subtle plant "defenses" are the shapes of the leaves, different foliage, and complex odours which, in mixed plantings, confuse insects.

Some plants seem to help each other. Radishes planted with cucumbers or with tomatoes help repel insects harmful to them. Radishes are more tender when grown near leaf lettuce. Lettuce is good grown with cucumbers and carrots. Tomatoes are compatible with onions, parsley and carrots.

Low bushy vegetables go with tall plants, making maximum use of sunlight and space. Carrots, lettuce and onions go well together. The onion, which also helps repel rabbits, reaches above the big, loose lettuce leaves, and carrot tops also get plenty of sun and help shade the lettuce. Lettuce is a perfect vegetable for interplanting, especially since it may be succession planted throughout the season. A light feeder, it makes good use of the soil between broccoli or tomatoes.

The American Indians interplanted corn, beans and squash. The squash was planted between hills of corn and the vines ran along the corn rows, shading out the weeds. Pole beans seeded after the corn started used the stalks to climb on and added nitrogen to the soil.

Even the shade thrown by one plant on the other can be helpful. There are many close associations of plants which grow better if planted in particular combinations. Some help in repelling bugs detrimental to the neighbouring crop, while others improve the flavour. Marigolds and nasturiums act as trap crops for nematodes and other insects. Colour, as well as odour, helps the gardener and sometimes even an orange coloured dish will attract insects.

Beans are a popular vegetable and some varieties have been grown for centuries. Starchier versions of our modern beans were a major crop of the ancient world. Montezuma Red beans have been grown in Mexico for over three thousand years. Beans were so commonplace that expressions arose: "I don't give a bean" and "It's not worth a hill of beans". A meal of beans was said to cleanse the skin as well as the belly. Summer savory eaten with dried beans helps cut the gas caused by eating the beans.

Cabbage and other members of the Brassica family are the oldest of the edible varieties of vegetables. There are some forty varieties of green, red, white, round, pointed or wrinkled cabbage, as well as broccoli, brussels sprouts and cauliflower.

The Greeks and Romans believed that if you ate cabbage during a banquet it would keep you from getting drunk. Cabbages contain B vitamins and these seem to have soothing and oxygenating qualities, welcomed when the mind is clouded by alcohol. Recent research in Texas shows that a substance extracted from cabbages is useful in the treatment of alcoholism.

Cabbage is not a sophisticated vegetable. The smell while it cooks is unpleasant and eating it may cause wind. Yet it is one of the most commonly grown vegetables. It is high in protein and low in calories.

The Celts may have been the ones to domesticate the wild cabbage. The Anglo-Saxons acquired a taste for all kinds of cabbage, which they called kale, so much so that they named February, the month they sowed it, "kale month".

According to a fourteenth century cookbook, cabbage should be cooked from early morning until suppertime over a good fire, and the resulting puree diluted with beef fat. On meat eating days it should be further embellished with pigeons, hares, sausages and bacon.

Cato, a classical writer, recommended eating raw cabbage. And a diet that contained cabbage was believed to prevent disease. Today, research shows that indeed, members of the cabbage family, especially brocolli, have medicinal properties and are recommended as a cancer preventative.

The cabbage family is rich in minerals, calcium, magnesium, sulphur and potassium, and in vitamins. The vitamin C content of cauliflower is greater than that of orange juice and cabbages were used in the eighteenth century on sailing ships on long voyages to help against scurvy. Cabbage family members are also said to be good for bones, skin, hair and nails. The leaves and juices applied externally were also said to have healing properties.

It is an old adage that babies are found in the cabbage patch, and an old custom was to bring a newly married couple cabbage soup the first thing in the morning after their bridal night. The linkage between the two is lost to antiquity.

Although the cabbage family is large, the potato ranks higher. Constituting about twenty five percent of the world's total vegetable food supply, there are said to be over three thousand varieties. The potato orignated in South America and was taken to Europe by the Spaniards and from there to Italy, the first European country to promote its growth. The English took the potato back to the New World with the early settlers. The name Irish became attached to the potato from stock brought from Ireland and raised in New Hampshire by settlers. This also distinguished the white potato from the sweet potato grown in the South.

Farmers in the mid-1800's averaged about eighty bushels of potatoes an acre. Eighty years ago the average was about one hundred bushels, and before the Second World War, one hundred twenty bushels. Then in the 1940's, it shot up and is now over three hundred bushels.

Varieties grown in the 1800's were unattractive, unproductive and highly susceptible to disease. Varieties kept "running out", and farmers waged a losing battle against the Colorado beetle which spread over the country. Many used poisonous Paris Green and London Purple insecticides applied in a mixture of ground plaster.

People today remember their Cape Breton Blacks, Calicoes and Early Rose potatoes. These old varieties have almost disappeared but many are being located and saved in genetic conservancy banks for the future.

There remains a strong demand for the old blue-black potatoes which are very dry (they don't get mushy in the pot) when cooked. A new arrival on the "blue market" is the Carib potato, much like the older varieties but bigger. However, some find that it doesn't overwinter as well as the older blue-blacks. The traditional blue-black is distinguished by its pecululiar shape with numerous protruding nobs which make it difficult to peel without wastage. It also has blue seams inside which boil out white. Enthusiasts, however, are happy to accept any disadvantage since "there's nothing better than boiled blue-blacks with salt cod". Other blue-blacks, though rarely found, are the totally black potatoes which boil to a blue colour but taste like any other potato, and the dry and once popular Calico potato.

Nova Scotians are often called "Bluenoses". This nickname is believed by some to be derived from potatoes originally imported from Britain, which were coloured at each end with a blue tint or, more likely, from the nobby blue-blacks. When these were, in turn, exported to other areas they were known as Nova Scotia Bluenoses. Another explanation is that it comes from the blue bows of Nova Scotian whaling ships.

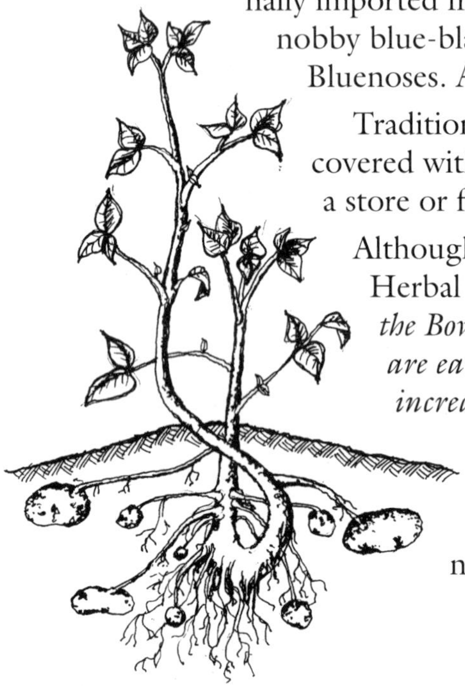

Traditionally people stored potatoes in a cellar with an earth floor or hole dug in the ground covered with straw, but today basements in modern homes are too warm, so it is better to buy from a store or farm market.

Although it was once believed that a person could catch leprosy from eating potatoes, an English Herbal book of 1710 gives other advice. *"The prepared roots of Potatoes of Virginia stop fluxes of the Bowels, nourish much, and restore Pining, Consumptions; being boiled, baked or roasted, they are eaten with Butter, Salt, Juice of Lemons and double refined Sugar, as common food; and then increase seed and provoke Lust, causing Fruitfulness in both sexes."*

There is nothing as delicious as a "feed" of tiny, new potatoes, boiled and served with butter and seasonings. Whether or not it provokes lust is for the consumer to decide. One popular Nova Scotian summer dish is "Squeal" or "Hodgepodge" made of baby new potatoes, peas, wax and/or green beans, smothered in cream. Not a dish for dieters.

Salads have long been popular summer dishes. To Louis XIV salads were moistening and refreshing as they liberated the stomach, were soothing and promoted sleep and appetite. Unlike potatoes they also tempered the *"ardours of Venus and quenched thirst"*.

Onions have an opposite effect. They are stimulating and said to sharpen vision and increase sexual prowess. Also rich in vitamin C, mineral salts and other trace elements, onions were included in sailors' rations for their long voyages. In earlier centuries onions were valuable and were used, along with garlic and parsley, to pay the labourers building the great pyramid in Egypt. Onions were a symbol of eternity and were set out with the mummies in their tombs. The ancient Egyptians also took their sacred oaths with their right hand on an onion. Onions were believed to keep away evil spirits and diseases. Garlic had the same effect. Garlic, they said, could protect people from bad air, the plague and vampires. Garlands of garlic were strung and worn while sleeping or hung over doorways as protection.

Garlic has been valued as a medicine to prevent, treat or cure a host of diseases from heart trouble and hypertension to dysentary and arthritis. Garlic is a source of vitamin C with fair amounts of vitamins A, B & G, lots of minerals, including sulphur, iron and calcium. It is rich in the trace element selenium, helps fight allergies and colds and is said to build the body's immune system, while cleansing and stimulating the digestive system.

Many believe it is a wide acting natural antibiotic and Celsius, the man who changed our thermometer, cited it as a cure for fevers. Pliny, the Roman naturalist, maintained that garlic was a cure for consumption and respiratory ailments. Today, research continues into the different aspects of garlic and scientists have discovered a way to "deodorize" it so that we can now buy odorless garlic oil capsules, garlic perles (tablets) and Keyolic capsules.

Queen Victoria's chef used to chew on a raw garlic clove and then breathe on the royal salad.

The Greek playwright, Aristophanes, wrote that athletes ate garlic to give them an extra boost in their competitions at the stadium. And he wrote, *"Take this garlic and swallow it without chewing. That when garlicked, my friend, you may fight better."* The ancient Romans gave garlic to their soldiers, to their game cocks, and to the harvest workers.

The prophet, Mohammed, said that garlic produced successful effects when it was applied to a poisonous snake bite or scorpion sting.

Garlic lovers say it can help anyone look better and feel younger and healthier. The Ancients thought it kept the body warm, brightened the face, and was an aphrodisiac.

Herbs have been used throughout the ages. The leaf, seeds or roots are still used in cooking. They also add fragrance to the air, serve as medicine and repel insects. Pots of basil on the windowsill help repel ants and flies. But custom also has it that when a woman put a pot of basil on her windowsill, she was ready to receive a suitor. Basil was also thought to cure infirmities of the heart and take away sorrow, making a man "merrie and glad".

Planting herbs is fairly simple. Called "simples" in the Middle Ages, they provided simple basic remedies. A simple was a medicine composed or concocted of one herb or plant. It is not necessary to have a whole garden set aside for herbs. A small, sunny corner near the kitchen door is convenient so that you can reach out and snip a few fresh herbs for cooking. Herbs can also be planted in clumps throughout both the vegetable and flower gardens or in a variety of intricate designs.

Folklore has grown with the herbs.

"Parsley, sage, rosemary and thyme..."

Parsley is more than just a decoration on dinner plates. The ancient Greeks used it to decorate the dinner guests because parsley was supposed to ensure tranquility and a good appetite, as well as sweetening the breath and pleasing the gods. Crowns of parsley were awarded to the winners of such games as the Olympics. The Greeks decorated their tombs with parsley and they used to say *"He has need now of nothing but a little parsley"*, meaning that he is dead.

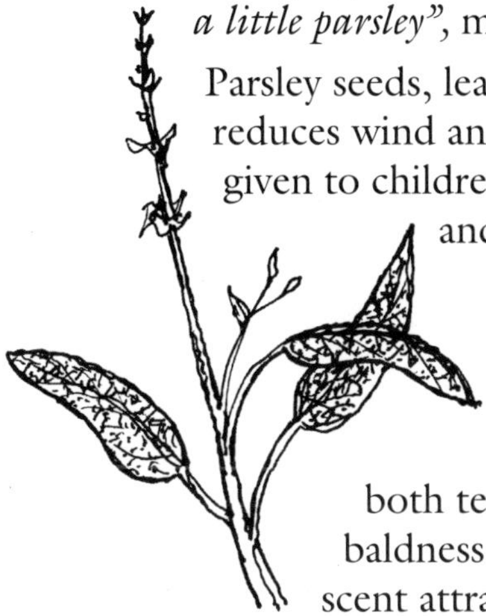

Parsley seeds, leaves and roots have all been used medicinally. Parsley helps stomach, liver and bladder ailments, it reduces wind and is generally helpful in aiding digestion. The distilled water of parsley was a familiar medicine given to children troubled with wind, or the "frets". Parsley is good raw, maintains its vitamins after being dried, and it is good cooked or fried in deep fat.

Sage was believed to help longevity and was equated with salvation or immortality. Used as a remedy for coughs, colds and fevers, and constitipation, it was also a general tonic. It made a good mouthwash, and crushed leaves scrubbed on the teeth benefitted both teeth and gums. Sage was used in the perfume industry and as a hair conditioner against baldness. It treated warts, epilepsy, insomnia, measles, seasickness and worms. In the garden its scent attracts bees. Sage is familiar as a herb in poultry seasoning and sausage flavoring.

Rosemary is associated with the Virgin Mary. The flowers are said to have taken their colour from her blue cloak when she threw it over a rosemary bush to dry. In Shakespeare's "Hamlet", Ophelia says, *"There's rosemary, that's for remembrance"*. The Greeks and Romans, believing that rosemary would quicken the mind and improve the memory, twined it in their hair. Rosemary was carried at weddings and funerals and used as a strewing herb, thought to have disinfectant qualities. It is good for digestion, stimulates circulation, deepens hair colour and is especially good eaten with lamb, fish and eggs.

Thyme is one of the ingredients in the cook's "bouquet garni", a small bunch of herbs for seasoning. Medicinally it has been an antiseptic and an ointment for pimples and, used in a tea sweetened with honey, helps promote sleep. Over the years thyme has symbolized courage, strength and happiness. In the Middle Ages ladies embroidered sprigs of thyme on the clothes of knights going off to the Crusades.

Flowers are special in any garden. They feed the spirit. Man cannot live by bread alone, the Bible says, and the thirteenth century Persian poet, Saadi, reflected this thought:

If of thy mortal goods thou art bereft,
And from thy slender store two loaves alone to thee are left,
Sell one, and with the dole
Buy hyacinths to feed thy soul.

Flowers have always been symbolic of emotion, but in the Victorian era, the use of the language of flowers reached its height. Flowers had subtle meanings, a language of their own. Instead of words, flowers were used to send messages. The specific language of flowers is lost today, but they remain a popular way of saying "Thank you", "Congratulations", "Hope you feel better" and "I love you".

There are other uses. We usually think of them in a garden, or arranged in a bridal bouquet or perhaps in a special arrangement on a table. But flowers are not only decorative. Daylillies, chrysanthemums, marigolds and others have been used in soups, for spices and syrups and in medicinal teas for years.

From early violets in the spring through to chrysanthemums in the fall, eating flowers was believed to increase longevity and reduce gray hairs. Flowers have been candied, pickled, dried and stewed. Before refrigeration people relied heavily on many seasonings. Herbs, spices and flowers all helped make the food more palatable.

In early pioneer days dried marigold petals were sold in the local country store "out of a barrel by the ounce" just like other herbs. There are many recipes for them. For example, they may be added to buns, cakes, drinks, eggs and pickles. They were used in soups to "comfort the heart". Like saffron, used mainly for its yellow colouring, marigold petals give the same golden colour and a pleasantly bitter taste. Petals also coloured butter and cheese.

During the American Civil War and during the First World War marigolds were mixed in lard or with alcohol for poultices on wounds. In the Second World War quantities of the flowers and leaves were gathered and used to induce perspiration to break a fever and to help bronchial complaints among the civilian population.

Nasturiums have also been popular. The "secret ingredient" in President Eisenhower's vegetable soup, a handful of chopped blossoms and stems were added for the last ten minutes of cooking.

Flowers are used in salads, sandwiches, souffles, jellies, in sauces for meat and fish, and as decorations for cakes and desserts. Crumpled dried petals of nastururiums were once a pepper substitute for ulcer sufferers.

Candied flowers can be made by coating them in egg white, covering with sugar, and drying. Violets, angelica, and roses were the most popular to "candy".

Along with the Bible, cookbooks were some of the earliest books to be printed(1475), but at first they were found only in royal households. Two early recipes: *"Take conies* (rabbits) *and smite them to pieces; seeth them in grease."* and *"Take chickens and ram them together, serve them broken"*.

JULY

This month, when the sun is the most potent, was appropriately named after the great Roman Emperor, Julius Ceasar. Other names included the Anglo-Saxon *"Hey Monath"* - *"Hay Harvest Month"* or *"Maedmonat"* - *"Meadow Month"*; the Welsh *"Gorfennaf"* - *"the Month of Completion"*; in Gaelic, *"am Mios buidhe"* - *"the Yellow Month"*; Celtic *"Hewimanoth"* - *"Hay Month"*; the Micmac *"Peskewiku's"* - *"Fur shedding"*; the full moon has been known as *"Buck Moon"* and *"Hay Moon"*.

How beautifully blue the sky,
The glass is rising very high,
Continue fine, I hope it may,
And yet it rained but yesterday.
To-morrow it may pour again
(I hear the country wants some rain),
Yet people say, I know not why,
That we shall have a warm July.

"Pirates of Penzance" by W.S. Gilbert

July 1 - Now known as Canada Day, started as Dominion Day, commemorating the confederation of the provinces into the Dominion of Canada in 1867. Celebrations include parades, picnics, and fireworks.

Red sky at night
Shepherd's delight;
Red sky in the morning
Shepherds take warning.

At this time of year continuous fair weather is now needed for haymaking.

St. Swithin's Day, if thou dost rain,
For forty days it will remain;
St. Swithin's Day, if thou be fine,
For forty days the sun will shine.

St. Swithin's Day, July 15, has been a special day for forecasting weather. If it rains on this day it will rain for forty days, or as one expression has it, *"If Mary goes over the hill on the fifteenth of July and gets her skirts wet, it will rain for forty days"*.

A halo around the moon is a sign of rain and when the wind blows and the undersides of the leaves are turned up, or when animals huddle in open fields or when mice dance on the hills, rain is on its way. When wind accompanies the storm, cats run and jump and the hens hide under shelter.

If the Moon shows a silver shield,
Be not afraid to reap your field.
But if she rises haloed round,
Soon we'll tread on deluged ground.

There are other signs of rain. Animals become agitated and disoriented. Sheep bleat and leap around, horses sneeze and rub their backs against the ground, cats and dogs race around, dogs eat grass, frogs and poultry make more noise, and swallows fly low. Bells can be heard from farther off than usual, lamps and candles sparkle more, and more soot falls down a chimney. When chairs and tables creak and crack and bubbles of coffee adhere to the cup forming a ring, it will rain. We too are animals and are affected by changes in atmosphere; our noses itch and our joints ache.

Early July marks the start of the "Dog Days of Summer". Today the expression means the lazy days of summer, but in the past the days were considered to be unhealthy and unlucky. At this time of year Sirius, the Dog Star, a brilliant, sparkling and scorching star, is ascendant in the sky. The "dog days" last until about the middle of August. In Greek times the star rose at dawn just before the sun marked the start of the hottest part of the summer. The Roman poet, Manilius, described the star as *"the dog with the blazing face. It barks forth flame and doubles the burning heat of the Sun."*

In 1729, *THE HUSBANDMAN'S PRACTICE* stated:

> *In these Dog Days it is forbidden by Astronomy to all Manner of People to be let Blood or take Physic. Yea, it is good to abstain all this time from Women...the kind of Star is broiling and burning as Fire. All this time the Heat of the Sun is so fervent and violent that Men's bodies at Midnight sweat as at Midday; and if they be hurt, they be more sick than at any other time, yea very near Dead. In these days all venomous serpents creep, fly and gender, so that many are annoyed thereby; in these times a Fire is good night and day, and wholesome, seeth well your meals and take heed of feeding violently.*

Today we are warned of the ill effects of too much sun but the ancients suggested taking a noontime siesta, wallowing in the mud or finding a rock to crawl under to keep cool.

Information and a warning from a *DIETARY HEALTH BOOK* in 1547 recommends, *"In summer, keep your neck and face from the sun, and wear gloves made of goatskins. And beware in standing or laying on the ground in the reflection of the sun, but be always movable. If you shall commune or talk with any man, stand not still in one place, especially if it be on the bare ground, or grass, or stones. Also beware in summer that you do not lie in old chambers that be not occupied, specially such chambers as mice, rats and snails resorteth unto."*

Yet more modern advice from 1617.

"In hot regions, to avoid the beams of the Sun, in some places (as in Italy) they carry Umbrels, or things like a little canopy over their heads but a learned Physician told me, that the use of them was dangerous, because they gather the heat into a pyramidal point, and thence cast it down perpendicularly upon the head."

There are many ways to tell if the weather will be hot: a white mist rising out of low ground or water, either before sunrise or after sunset; birds flying high in the air; cobwebs on the grass; lots of lightning bugs; and clouds of flies playing in the sunlight before sunset.

Farmers are particularly glad to see the sun at haymaking time. And as the old adage goes "*Make hay while the sun shines*". Work starts as soon as the sun dries off the dew and continues until evening, although Belcher's *FARMER'S ALMANACK* admonishes farmers to *"do your mowing early in the week, so that your hay will not have to lie over Sunday washing in the rain or bleaching in the sun"*.

A short handled sickle or a long handled sythe were used to cut the grass and grain and a hay rake to untangle and turn the hay to dry; a hay fork was used to pitch hay into a wagon or feed box.

Haymaking started about the middle of July. Farmers would help each other, going around from farm to farm, with horses and wagons and, later, trucks.

After the hay was cut, it was raked, stacked with a pitchfork into piles about four to five feet high, and scraped down the sides, so if it rained the rain would run off the stack and most of the hay would stay dry. The next morning farmers would shake the stacks apart and open them out so the hay could dry further.)

There was quite an art to "staking" the load, building and strengthening it, and pitching on more hay. The faster a person worked the sooner the job was finished. The men threw the hay up to "make a load of hay". Then, when the hay was dry, two poles were shoved underneath the stack, lifted and carried to the barn. The stored hay must be dry or it will gradually heat up, smoulder and catch on fire.

Women raked the hay that missed being tossed on the load. They also cleaned the stables, spread new bedding and let the animals in and out.

Hay balers or hay pressers were first built in the 1850's, reducing the time and effort spent on haymaking.

Although little smells as sweet as freshly mown hay, stacking the hay in the barn is dusty work. A person sneezes and the hay is scratchy as it gets in the hair and down the shirt. Nevertheless, it is great fun to climb on top of a haystack and slide down. Today, haymaking is easier, with machines doing most of the work, but some of the fun has been lost.

Many customs surrounded the ritual of making hay. It was hard work, and the easing of the burden became something of a competition. Whoever finished first would make "a man of hay", although sometimes the hay was made into the shape of a woman and decorated with flowers, ribbons, and straw ornaments. In the old days this "man" might be placed in the barn to keep the mice away. It was good luck to be the one who made the man of hay. They said that whoever did would be married before the next harvest. It was also good luck for the animals and was kept and fed to them at Christmas. As a charm to ensure a good crop the following year, the last sheaf of this year's harvest was made unusually large.

It was also good luck to make a wish on a load of hay.

Through all the pleasant meadow-side
The grass grew shoulder-high,
Till the shining scythes went far and wide
And cut it down to dry.

These green and sweetly smelling crops
They led in waggons home;
And they piled them here in mountain tops
for mountaineers to roam...

O what a joy to clamber there,
O what a place to play,
With the sweet,the dim, the dusty air,
The happy hills of hay.

"The Hayloft" by Robert Louis Stevenson

Harvest time has always been important. When crops failed, starvation lay ahead. Therefore a good harvest was good reason to celebrate. Not so many years ago in Cape Breton after haymaking farmers would "make a big dance" in a big outhouse (any building other than the house) with cornmeal on the floor. Dances were a major social event. People still remember saying the Rosary before going to a dance because they would not be awake enough when they got home early next morning - sometimes they only reached home in time to milk the cows. Some, in fact, were often so tired that they even prayed for rain.

Frequently, during haymaking, a deer was hunted, butchered and kept on ice. Ice houses were small outbuildings where large squares (cakes) of ice cut in the winter were stored with straw or sawdust to keep the ice preserved. An earthern floor was covered with loose rock for drainage and with a twelve inch layer of sawdust or a thicker layer of hay or cut straw. The walls were of rough planks and often there was no roof but instead a deep covering of sawdust or hay. Hay, straw or wood chips also made a good insulation in the walls. This was one of the early means of refrigeration. Commercial ice plants developed when the ice was needed in various fish plants, as well as in the home kitchen icebox.

In 1896 advice was given on how to live in the summer.

> *"Ice water kills more persons than strychnine. It should be drunk in great moderation and slowly sipped, a mouthful at a time - never gulped. It should be absolutely avoided at meals. Taken in the mouth directly after hot food it cracks the enamel of the teeth, and entering the stomach, it chills the natural fluids, so that they are unfitted for the work of digestion, thus laying the foundation for a thousand evils.*
>
> *The use of moderately cold water not only averts these, but slakes the thirst much better than the ice-cold fluid. Avoid beverages that contain much sugar, acidulated drinks are better. Alcoholic stimulants in such weather are in the highest degree dangerous, over-heating the system and deranging all the bodily functions. If one absolutely needs stimulants a glass of cold tea or coffee, plain or with soda water, slowly imbibed, will key you up to your work better than whiskey."*

For most illnesses people relied on themselves and their various folk remedies, calling on the doctor only in dire emergency. When needed, emergency operations were held on kitchen tables. People believed that if they went to hospital it was to die.

Today many feel that these remedies were nonsense, but research has begun to recognize that some are valid.

In summer plants were gathered for medicinal purposes. The more common plants are still found in the woods and fields although they are now considered weeds in cultvated areas.

A Brigade Order in 1758 concerning the reduction of Louisbourg Fortress included the following:

"Experience having discovered that ginger and sugar mixed with the water of America prevents the effects of it, and preserve the men from fevers and fluxes better than anything else found out, Br. General Lawrence does therefore recommend the use of this discovery to the Troops in the strongest manner."

A miscellany of old remedies.

Wounds and infections:

Various poultices: a poultice of plantain leaves, of bread, sugar and milk, or of bruised leaves of chicory.

A poultice made with hot water and crushed flax seeds or one made with the roots of buttercups or violets was used for boils or drawing out splinters.

Highly recommended as a poultice was cow manure mixed with linseed meal and warmed.

For bandages pieces of birchbark or brown paper were used.

Bleeding:

A tea made from the seeds and leaves of shepherd's purse was said to stop bleeding. It was also used during child-birth for contracting the uterus. An external wash was used for bruises.

Cobwebs or yarrow flowers were applied to a wound to help stop bleeding. The ancient Greek hero, Achilles, was said to have used yarrow to stem the bleeding arrow wounds of his men. More recently, a tea made from the leaves of alfalfa stopped bleeding and a tea of lupines stopped internal hemorrhaging. A piece of copper put under the tongue helped stop a nosebleed.

Burns:

Red clover was used for burns, athletes foot and sores and also externally as a cancer remedy. The crushed seeds of wild mustard, purslane or goldenrod were used in a poultice for burns. Boiled tea or wet tea grounds were also useful.

Toothaches:

Toothaches were a common ailment and there were a number of ways to treat them. A person could make an infusion of lemon balm, chew yarrow leaves, put mare's milk (or in the event there was none, regular cow's milk) against the tooth, put powdered cloves directly onto the sore tooth, or some nicotine on a little piece of cotton on a straw (like a modern Q tip) after cleaning a pipe. A verse from the Bible written on a piece of paper and folded into a small square, sewn in cloth and tied around the neck or a bag of coarse salt, heated and laid against the check were other remedies.

Headaches:

For a headache brown paper or cloth in vinegar was tied over the forehead, as in the nursery rhyme about Jack and Jill.

Then up Jack got and home did trot,
As fast as he could caper;
Went to bed to mend his head
With vinegar and brown paper.

An infusion of fresh lavendar could also be used as a cold compress, and slices of cucumbers placed over the eyes could relieve a headache.

Stomachaches & nausea:

Infusions or teas of basil leaves, peppermint or lemon balm, wild strawberries, water with a pinch of baking soda, lavendar, lupines, or purslane. Caraway seed tea and alderbark tea also helped relieve cramps.

Diarrhea:

Milk boiled with an iron nail in it was useful, as was pepper and cold water, a little flour dissolved in water, or nutmeg boiled in milk.

Colds and Coughs:

See February.

Miscellaneous:

Dried eelskin wrapped around a sore ankle or wrist brings relief.

The seeds of Queen Anne's Lace were used as a "morning after" contraceptive. The plant is very similar to the Poison Hemlock, which was also used as a contraceptive because it was believed to be an anti-aphrodisiac. It was also believed to be a cancer remedy. Alfalfa was thought helpful against cancer, diabetes, alcoholism, and arthritis.

To get rid of warts a person could go to the graveyard at midnight, kill a frog or spit three times, but it was easier, and just as reliable, to cut a raw potato, rub it on the wart and then bury the potato, or rub the wart with a piece of meat or castor oil.

For hiccups one can hold one's breath, be suddenly frightened, drink water from the opposite side of a glass, breathe into a paper bag, or boil dill seeds and leaves in wine and drink it.

A sty could be removed by rubbing it with a gold ring.

Sheep manure tea for the measles or as a general cure-all, mare's milk for T.B. and whooping cough.

Tuberculosis, the "*Great White Plague*", *"causes more deaths than any other disease that afflicts the human race. It kills more people than war, famine, or any of the raging plagues or pestilences that startle our imagination by their fearful ravages. It is the most widespread of all fatal diseases; no country is free from it, no age exempt, no class of society immune."*

"Throughout the world one death in every six or seven is caused by tuberculosis in one form or another... Of the seven and a half millions of inhabitants living in Canada to-day (1912), a million are doomed to die of consumption." Closer to home, at that time in Cape Breton, an average of about two hundred fifty people died each year from T.B.

But the numbers dying of the disease were only part of the story. *"For every one consumptive who dies in any given year many times that number exist as living victims of the disease, leading a life of suffering and distress".*

With all the incurable diseases, as well as the less fatal illnesses, it is little wonder that people would try anything that might help.

Then, as now, asthma was a worry. One help for a child with asthma was to blindfold him, take him to a tree, where a hole was bored at his height and a lock of his hair put in the hole. This hole was plugged up and the patient led away, hopefuly to outgrow the asthma. A person could also get rid of a fever by putting some of his hair and nail clippings in a hole in a tree and then plugging it. Children themselves were put in a large hole in a tree to get better. Or one could try to scrape the illness off by passing through a cleft in the tree.

In place of a tree a wooden door was sometimes used. A hole was bored and locks of hair and nail clippings enclosed, then plugged. This was to help nosebleeds, asthma, bronchitis, croup and colic. It was a folk medicine practiced from Nova Scotia to the American midwest. In Lunenburg County a baby with pleurisy was passed under a wooden leg of a table for a cure.

These tree remedies go back to the ancient belief that trees were sacred and had potent healing powers. Relatively recently, these beliefs in healing properties of trees have moved from the trees to wooden doors and table legs.

Drinking or bathing in mineral water from special mineral springs, like the one at Glengary, near Big Pond, or the Roman mineral springs at Bath in England, helped a variety of ailments including rheumatism.

A Cape Breton medicine shelf often contained bottles of camphor, smelling salts, and Minard's Linament, which was "hot as fire" and "like a knife in your heart". A little put in hot milk was used for everything from cuts and burns to upset stomachs and cramps.

One of summer's evening chores remains finding the cows, which have been pasturing and roaming the fields and woods all day, and to bring them home for milking. Perhaps, if one was a lover, one would not want the cows to be readily found, for as the Elizabethan playwrights Beaumont and Fletcher wrote *"Kiss till the cow comes home"*.

It was not only rural people who kept cows. At the turn of this century many people in towns also kept three or four. The cows wandered freely, becoming nuisances at times. They were known to wander at night and the sound of their bells kept people awake. In Sydney and other towns newspapers frequently included notices for missing cows.

Many farm families had about a dozen cows. The milk was kept in a cool place, such as a well house. About sixty pounds of butter could be churned each week from the cream. Some of the butter was salted down for the winter (using about one ounce of salt per pound), while other butter was sold to stores, making an important contribution to the farm income.

An easy way to separate cream is to let the milk set for a while, so that the cream rises to the surface and can be then skimmed off.

For quicker results milk was put in a separator, a machine that spun the entire cream out of the milk by centrifugal force. The rich cream came out of one pipe and the thinner milk out of another. Butter was made in a wooden plunger churn, with the plunger moving up and down for hours.

Cold water was hauled from a spring or well. The water had to be cold to make the butter firm. For as many as five times, water was put on the butter to rinse out the buttermilk, which was used for cooking and drinking. The butter was put into moulds or patted into small loaf shapes.

The skim milk was set out to sour for a couple days, then warmed up, often along with a little sweet whole milk, and the heat separated the curds, or cottage cheese, from the whey. Some rennet was added, the curds gathered up and strained, and about a half cup of salt was added to each gallon of curds. The remaining milk went to the pigs.

Crab and lobsters, caught during the fullness of the moon, were believed to be fatter.

Indians, at night, used to fish or lure lobsters to shore by the light from burning torches, then spear them in the shallows. Lieutenant B.W.A. Sleigh, stationed at Sydney Garrison in 1846, wrote, *"Of an evening, from my bedroom window, I would be attracted by a gleam of light passing along the wall, and on looking out numerous canoes were to be seen, with pine-torches burning, while the Indians were spearing salmon, which are attracted to the surface by the light passing over it."*

Lobsters were plentiful. Catching them, for some people, was almost incidental to a night of fun. There are stories of lobsters being piled several feet high on the beach after a storm. These were a nuisance, damaging fish nets. As late as the 1850's, they were often used as a fertilizer. The lobster industry began at this time.

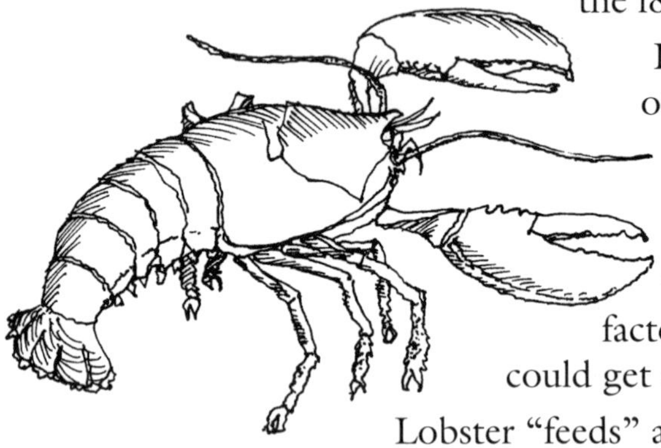

Lobster canning season was from mid-May to mid-July. Canning factories sprang up on the coast of Cape Breton at Wreck Cove, Alder Point, Port Morien, and Grand Etang. At one point at the factory at Big Bras d'Or there were as many as sixty girls and eighteen men working. Many local girls and women worked in these plants, but often people from other parts of the island, and as far away as Guysborough, came to work, and would only be able to travel back home on an occasional Sunday. The factories began to be shut down at the end of the 1930's and early 1940's when fishermen could get a better price for the larger lobsters by shipping direct to the States.

Lobster "feeds" are now popular summer events. The lobsters are good eaten with butter, and nothing else is needed to make the meal a success.

The swordfish industry did not begin until the 1920's. It started locally in the Ingonish area, where there were bigger boats, and the fish were caught, salted and sent to the States. Rum-running boats, anchored off Glace Bay, often did double duty. They caught the swordfish after they had unloaded the rum, putting the fish on ice and taking the catch to Boston. When the rum-running era ended boats were more extensively used for sword fishing.

AUGUST

August

This month is named for the Roman Emperor, Augustus. It is also known in Gaelic *"Ab Lugnasda" - "Month of the Lammas Festival";* in Anglo/Saxon, *"Weodmonath" - "Month of Weeds";* in Celtic *"Aranmanoth" - "Corn Ears Month"; "Month of the harvest";* Micmac *"Kisikwekewiku's" - "Growing Season Complete";* while the full moon has been called the *"Sturgeon"* or *"Corn Moon"*. The reigning goddess is Ceres or Demeter, the goddess of the harvest.

Simple Simon met a pieman
Going to the fair.
Says Simple Simon to the pieman,
Let me taste your ware.

The first of August was once called Lammas Day, from "Loaf-mass", the festival of harvest's beginning, when the first cut sheaf of "corn" (corn in England is used to describe any grain) or bread made from it, was blessed and offered in churches.

In Highland Scotland it was a festival of the Celtic god Lugnasadhe, celebrated with gatherings, sports and great bonfires. It was also a time when spirits walked abroad and hence a good time to divine the future.

Rents were paid on Lammas Day, fences were pulled down and the public had access to private property.

The first of August is today a bank or civic holiday and the harvesting connections have disappeared.

One of the best known myths of agriculture is that of Demeter and her daughter, Persephone. Demeter was the Greek goddess of agriculture and the harvest, in charge of cultivated soil, especially land that produced grain. Married to Zeus, the king of the gods, they had a daughter, Persephone. This alliance of the god of heaven with the earth goddess caused the fertility of the earth. But, Persephone's uncle, Hades, ruler of the underworld, the land of the dead, fell in love and abducted her. Demeter travelled the earth in sorrow looking for her daughter. She no longer blessed the harvest and the whole earth became unproductive, infertile and sterile until her daughter returned. Zeus ordered Hades to give the girl back, but it was too late. Any who crossed the threshold of the underworld could not return if they had eaten anything. And Persephone had eaten a pomegranite seed. A compromise was reached. If Demeter would go back to caring for the earth and crops, Persephone need only stay half the year in the underworld and the other half she could be with her mother. That is why half the year the earth is sterile and unproductive; when Persephone leaves the underworld to be with her mother, spring and fertility return with her.

The goddess, Ceres, was the Roman equivalent of Demeter. It is from Ceres that we get our name for cereal, from grain which is a basic crop for us and the principal crop under the care of Ceres and Demeter.

You ought to have seen what I saw on my way
To the village, through Patterson's pasture today:
Blueberries as big as the end of your thumb,
Real sky-blue, and heavy, and ready to drum
In the cavernous pail of the first one to come!
And all ripe together, not some of them green
And some of them ripe! You ought to have seen!...

I wish I knew half what the flock of them know
Of where all the berries and other things grow,
Cranberries in bogs and raspberries on top
Of the boulder-strewn mountain,
and when they will crop....

We'll pick in the Pattersons' pasture this year.
We'll go in the morning, that is, if it's clear,
And the sun shines out warm: the vines must be wet.
It's so long since I picked I almost forget
How we used to pick berries: we took one look round,
Then sank out of sight like trolls underground...

"Blueberries" by Robert Frost

Summer is the time for wild berry picking. First there are wild strawberries, followed by wild raspberries. Then come blueberries. People came from the immediate neighborhood and from nearby towns to pick. Picking was a chore that had to be done, so it was made into a party. Children sold their berries and used the money for school supplies and clothes and the money also helped their parents pay for pots, pans and rugs. The pickers left home early in the morning, taking with them a large pail and small dishes. Two or three trips were made each season. People could also get fifty cents a gallon for wild strawberries which had been picked earlier, and a good picker could gather up to fifteen or twenty gallons of blueberries and one hundred sixty quarts of strawberries a year.

THE GREAT MOUSE PLAGUE

Farmers have always had to deal with rats and mice. *"A female Mouse having free liberty to litter, within less than half a year she hath brought forth a hundred and twenty young ones." (1607).* Rodents have always caused damage. Everyone knows of the Black Death, spread by rats. No greater calamity afflicted the world as we know it than the Black Death of the fourteenth century. There are estimates that more than a third of the western world died horribly from this plague, which continued to threaten the world for five hundred years.

Born in Central Asia, it followed the caravans along the old Silk Road into Asia Minor and from there on boats into western Europe. In came in bacillus in the stomachs of rats. Fleas from the sick and dying rats needed a new host and so they went onto man. It was called the Black Death and in just a few years it killed from seventeen to perhaps more than thirty million people. Attacking both rich and poor alike, it wrought political and social change and terrified mankind as thousands died choking upon blood, afflicted by bulbous swellings around the groin and armpits, and blackened stinking flesh.

What caused it? We know that it was the carried by rats. But for the medieval world there were other causes. The Pope's physician was convinced that it began with "a grand conjunction of Saturn, Jupiter and Mars under the sign of Aquarius". Other doctors held comets responsible. But the public generally knew better. It came in the thick mists in the air and the answer was to fumigate that air. So people wore garlands of thyme, rosemary and other herbs or carried them in their pockets to counter the poisonous mists.

Surviving from these times is the nursery rhyme, "Ring a ring of roses, a pocket full of poses, tish a tish a, we all fall down."

There were other ways of avoiding the plague. People from the cities fled to the country, while country people abandonned their villages and farms. In response to the emotional panic, many were led by the figure Death in bizarre dances of death in cemetaries. Others by the hundreds and thousands, wandered two by two in long processions from vil- lage to village. Bypassing the clergy, who seemded unable to give them spiritual comfort, they took on a direct involvement with God as they punished themselves for their sins, believing these had brought the plague. These people flayed themselves by whipping their bare skin with a scourge, a stick from which three tails with large knots penetrated by iron spikes.

Some tried to hide in their homes; some dedicated themselves to drink and sex. For others, ab-staining from sexual intercourse was believed to help. Cursing or political arguments were advised against. The very rich tried eating a tonic made with liquid gold and powdered emeralds. Nothing seemed to work.

Infected houses and plague victims were marked with a red cross.

It suddenly ended, though the reason for that too remains a mystery. Over the centuries though it would recur, for example, in the Great Plague if the mid-seven-teenth century. To this day, in the village of Eyam in Derbyshire in England, there is an annual commemoration service for the victims, where nine out of every ten in the village had died. The plague still lingers on. In India, at the turn of this century, many thousands died and even in this decade there have been isolated cases reported in North America.

People also know of the town of Hamlin and its rescue from a plague of rats by the Pied Piper. Few know, however, of a terrible plague of mice suffered by the people of the Maritimes.

The summer of 1815 was particularly destructive. As reported later by C.J. MacChesney, the old nursery rhyme which tells the story of the three blind mice, ends with the question, "Did you ever see such a sight in your life?" The farmers of Pictou, Antigonish and Colchester counties would certainly have answered positively to that question back in 1815. Instead of merely three blind mice, the sight which they witnessed was more likely three hundred thousand and

none of them blind! For the woods and the fields were literally alive with the hurrying, tumbling, squeaking pests that destroyed everything edible in sight.

"During the War of 1812 certain coastal sections of the Maritimes were enjoying the prosperity which characterizes war years. Money was flowing in through the war expenditures of the British Government and from the sale of prize ships and cargoes brought in by privateers and cruisers. Ship repairs, sales of materials and of ships' supplies commanded such high prices that the farmers neglected their planting and harvesting.

"However, the money that came so easily went just as quickly so that when, in 1815, peace returned they were obliged to turn back to their farms as the source of their livelihood.

"While the whole country was feeling the effects of the depression, to add to their worries, that year also brought the destructive visitation of the mice. The rodents swarmed over the farms which had been neglected and offered little in the way of food, and raced on to the abundant farms of the diligent farmers of the district. When they passed on, those who had laboured long, hard and earnestly were no better off than those who had not worked at all.

"By the end of the winter of 1815 the mice, which had not appeared in any unusual numbers during the previous year, had become so numerous that the sugar makers in the maple woods were having trouble. The little animals were clustering in and around the sap buckets, creeping into the troughs, the vats, and among the supplies in the camps.

"A nuisance at sugar time, at planting time they became a menace. The farmers were amazed and horrified to discover that the woods and fields were overrun by thousands upon thousands of a species slightly larger that the ordinary field mouse, blackish in color with short legs and flat paws.

"Not only were the creatures terribly destructive, but they were actually fierce! So fierce, in fact, that in many cases they turned upon the farmers' cats and fought them off.

"It is recorded that at Merigomish where the mice had not shown themselves in any great numbers in the fields, a man who had cleared a spot of ground near the woods took 4 bushels of oats and went forth to sow. With the very firsthandful of grain thrown, the mice came swarming from the woods and ate each kernel as it fell to the ground. The startled farmer looked about him. As far as his eyes could see the field was alive with mice. Realizing the hopelessness of the situation he gave the rest of the grain to the pests and returned home in disgust.

"Strange as it may seem, some areas were left untouched by the mice. Here crops were planted and carefully tended. Then, when the harvest was ready, as if by a given signal the pests came pouring out of the woods and onto the farmlands in such numbers that it was useless to try to cope with them.

"Over acres and acres they moved like regiments of soldiers, leaving not one stalk of grain behind them - not even one kernel of wheat. An acre was demolished in 3 days, whole fields in a week. While thousands were busy eating everything on the surface thousands more burrowed into the earth and ate the root crops.

"Dogs, cats and martens gorged themselves upon the marauders, but hundreds of thousands still remained. When the frantic farmers banded together and dug deep ditches, hurrying hordes fell unto the trenches and drowned by the thousands until the water-filled cuts were jammed with them. But the living crossed over the dead bodies of their companions and into the abundant fields beyond.

"Then, as suddenly as they had come, the mice disappeared. As the weather grew cold in the autumn, the mice became slow and lazy - scarcely able to crawl. They died by the thousands. Their bodies were everywhere underfoot, and the smell of decaying flesh fouled the air.

"Millions of them pressed down to the water's edge, as if playing a game of "Follow the leader", and drowned. Long lines of bodies formed ridges like seaweed along the shores. They left in their wake bare fields, empty barns and pillaged houses.

"In Prince Edward Island there is a town named Souris - the French word for mouse. This name commemorates similar depredations by mice in this province many years before Nova Scotia's ordeal. Between 1724 and 1738 the settlers suffered from 3 destructive visits of the mice. After they had eaten their way through spring sowing at Three Rivers to harvest at Malpequa, destroying everything in their path so that the settlers faced starvation, they poured over the dykes and drowned.

"But in 1815 the disappearance of the mice did not mean that the settlers' troubles were over, for the "Year of the Mice" was followed by the "Year of the Frost". A year in which all the harvest was destroyed followed by a year without a sufficient warm weather to raise new crops left a large number of people in a suffering condition.

"On June 4 of 1816, the year without a summer, a great snowstorm swept over the country and the Maritime provinces were covered with a mantle of snow a foot deep. Within 2 weeks a second storm followed, in which several people caught in it, were frozen to death.

"July brought little relief. On July 4 there was ice one-fourth of an inch thick. August was even worse, for in that month ice formed to the depth of half an inch. The first two weeks of September were milder, but the remainder of the month, and the two which followed, were bitterly cold. A remarkably mild December was slight consolation for a lost summer.

"Many theories were advanced as to the cause of the unusual weather. The farmer, fearing that the two successive calamities might be punishment for the neglect of their land during the war, went diligently to work."

Little wonder that mice are signs of ill omen, hunger or impending death, with large numbers of them signalling war. Like the legend of rats and mice leaving a sinking ship, they are also said to flee a house in which death is imminent. Oddly enough, white mice are a symbol of good luck.

Mice have been found in the stomachs of children of ancient Egypt. Closer to our time, some people, including the English and the Pennsylvania Dutch, used mouse pie or fried mice as a cure for bedwetting. Cooked mice were also recommended for smallpox, whooping cough and measles. Mouse ashes with honey were recommended for an earache, and if used as a mouthwash, helped sweeten breath. An English cookbook published in the First World War, fearing still worse to come, had a recipe for rat pie.

Farmers resorted to various means to get rid of mice and rats. Even guns and sticks were used. But there is another method. A treatise on farming in ancient Greece suggests,

> "Take a sheet of paper and write on it as follows 'I adjure you, ye mice here present, that ye neither injure me nor suffer another mouse to do so. I give you yonder field' (here the field is specified) 'but if ever I catch you here again, by the Mother of the Gods, I will rend you in 7 pieces.' Write this and stick it on a rough stone in the field before sunrise, taking care to keep the written side up."

In France, written in Latin, another letter:

"'Male rats and female rats, I conjure you, by the great God, to go out of my house, out of all my habitations, to betake yourselves to such and such a place, there to end your days.' Then write the same words on pieces of paper, fold them up and place one of them under the door by which the rats are to leave and the other on the road which they are to take. Do at sunrise."

"Sandwich, New Hampshire. May 9,1845

...."my patience is all gone. I cannot find words bad enough to express what I feel, you black devils you are, gnawing at our corn while we sleep....Now, spirits of the bottomless pit, depart from this place with all speed! Look not back! Begone, or you are ruined! We are preparing water to drown you, fire to roast you, cats to catch you, and clubs to maul you. Unless you...quit here and go to Ike Nute's farm...a hint to the wise is sufficient..."

Mrs Weed

However, a later writer, the caretaker of a summer property in New England, believed he could catch more rats with honey than vinegar. The following letter was rolled up, greased, and left by the entrance of a rat hole in the wall of the house.

"Maine, Oct 31, 1888

Messrs. Rats & Co.–

Having taken quite a deep interest in your welfare in regard to
your winter quarters I thought I would drop you a few lines
which might be of some considerable benefit to you in the future,
seeing that you have pitched your winter quarters at the summer
residence of #1 Seaview St. I wish to inform you that you will
be very much disturbed during the cold winter months as I am
expecting to be at work through all parts of the house, shall take
down ceilings, take up floors, and clean out every substance that
would serve to make you comfortable, likewise there will be nothing
left for you to feed on, as I shall remove every eatable
substance; So you had better take your abode elsewhere, I will
here refer you to the farm of #6 Incubator St. where you will
find a splendid cellar well filled with vegetations of all kinds,
besides a shed leading to a barn, with a good supply of grain,
where you can live snug and happy. Shall do you no harm if you
heed my advice; but if not shall employ "Rough on Rats (a poison)"

Yours...

From the 1890's, until the Great Depression and drought in the west brought an end to the annual excursions, men from the Maritimes went west in droves on special Harvest Trains to help with the harvest.

Changing to the special "Harvest Train" at Saint John, an average of sixty five people were crammed like cattle into each of the eleven cars. There was one toilet in each car and one small tank of water for drinking with another for washing and cooking. The railway cars, with the exception of one with the other passengers, were cleaned out only once on the five to seven day trip to the wheatfields.

Cape Bretoners, known as the "wild men from the Far East", for their brawling, were blamed for much of the damage to the rail cars. As one critic commented, the rail cars were *"filled with a howling, swearing, singing mob. Drunken fiddlers squeaked for dear life with drunken tunes on drunken fiddles, while drunken dancers danced to the drunken music. The air was foul in the extreme and filled with the odor of stale tobacco smoke."*

Summertime is also the season of laziness and fun. Boating and swimming have always been popular. It is hard to believe today that Sydney Harbour was once a receational heaven. Sailing and yachting remain popular, but years ago rowboats and canoes were also seen, especially around the Wentworth Park area and across the Harbour at Westmount's Crawley Creek. Early in this century crowds also went to Crawley's Creek to swim. Below where Keddy's Motel now stands there was another great place to swim, Nelgah Beach, complete with a pavillion for dances. People also swam across the Harbour to North Sydney.

Two-day picnics, usually held at the beginning of August, were used by the churches as fund raisers. Stages were set up outside for dancing and young hardwood was cut and used for fences and leafy bowers in the picnic grounds. Special picnic trains left the Sydney area for Iona and Louisbourg, two favorite picnic spots.

These picnics started at about ten in the morning and continued into the evening. There were games, softball, running races, and fish ponds, where for twenty five cents one threw in a line and tried to catch a prize. Fiddlers and bagpipers played for listening or dancing. Food was donated, and a meal cost a dollar. Ice cream was made by hand in three or four special freezer machines, packed with ice. Small cones cost five cents; large ones a dime. Homebrew was also in evidence. Sometimes from four to five hundred dollars was made from all the sales.

Mid-summer was the best time for stripping birchbark from trees because it peeled off more easily. Indians made a variety of items with the birchbark, including baskets, small decorative teepees, cradles, and canoes. Axe handles, rustic furniture and baskets of all shapes and sizes were made from local hardwoods.

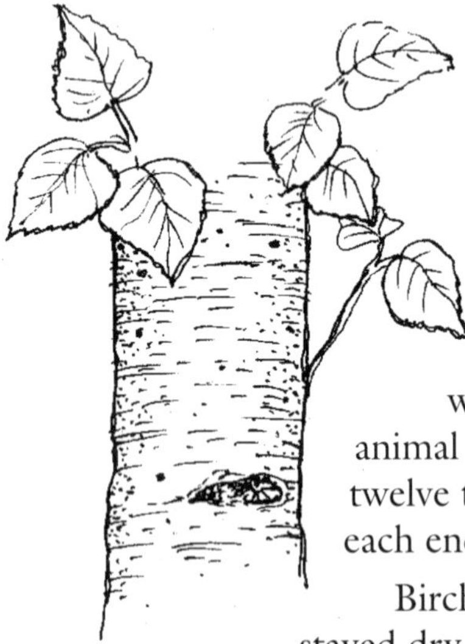

Years ago rolls of birchbark covered pole frameworks for wigwams. Pieces were stitched together with yellow birch "string" and each piece held stretched out at the ends by splits of white maple. Five or more poles were tied togther at the top and pulled into a wide circle to make a cone shaped structure. A slender hoop braced the inside. Thinner poles were also placed between the five main poles and tied to the hoop. Then sheets of birchbark were sewn together and placed over the poles in overlapping rows from the bottom up. Designs were often painted on the birchbark. An opening at the top let out smoke from the fire while another opening at the side was the doorway. For insulation, the wigwam might be covered with mats woven from reeds, or animal skins or canvas. The floor was covered with evergreen boughs and furs. The average wigwam held twelve to fifteen people. If a larger one was needed, it was oblong in shape with two fireplaces, one at each end.

Birchbark was also used by the early settlers. Strips covered the gaps between boards of house wallls. It stayed dry and it kept out drafts.

Strips of yellow birch were made into brooms or twisted to create a resilient rope. Yellow birch was also bent to form the bows of snowshoes, with maple being carved for the toe and heel beam. These were filled in with lighter rawhide straps which had been cut from cured cowhides.

The early settlers built simple log cabins. The rafters were covered with the bark of the spruce trees and the chinks in the wall filled with moss and mud.

Acadian houses were often built with the barn attached to the house which made winter care of the stock easier.

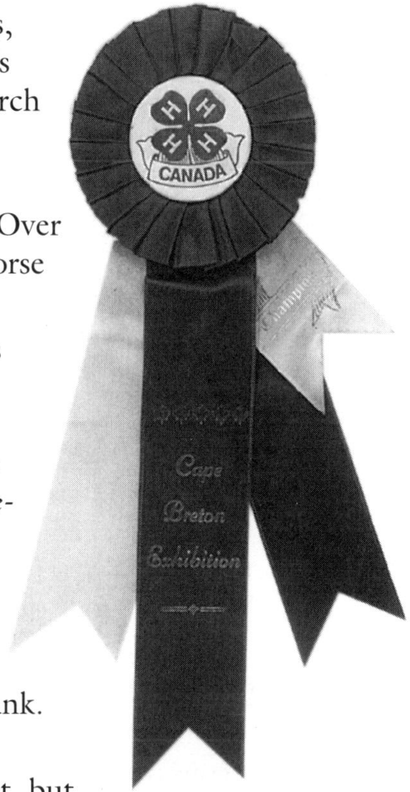

Fairs have been held since the earliest times. Ancient Greeks and Romans had their fairs, attended by a variety of traders, but later fairs were largely connected with religious festivals and were associated with the period of a Saint's feast day and held in the precincts of a church or abbey.

Because fairs were soon forbidden on religious sites they moved out and expanded. In England, between 1199 and 1483, twenty eight thousand grants were given to hold fairs. Over the centuries they have evolved into markets for specialties - in Bristol, for example, the Horse Fair, in Nottingham a goose fair and in Gloucester a fair for butter and cheese.

Some fairs, for example, the Charlton Fair on St Luke's Day (18 October) had customs evocative of a pagan past. (See 14 February and December - Mummering) Thousands of fairgoers wore horns on their heads. The men dressed as women and lashed out at the real women with bunches of furze (a prickly evergreen shrub). They said, *"All's fair at the horn fair."* Said a writer of the period, *"they involved too great an element of coarseness, if not something worse."*

Paid-for entertainment was added to fairs. Today we have roundabouts and other amusements. Popular near London at the Greenwich Fair, in addition to the general frivolity, was the use of a telescope with which, for a half-penny, you could look at the distant St Paul's Cathedral or, far more popular, pirates hanging in chains along the riverbank. Soon entertainment was taking precedence over agricultural marketing.

Exhibitions and fairs here were usually held in September and October, after the harvest, but today most are in August.

As I was going to Banbury,
Upon a summer's day,
My dame had butter, eggs and fruit,
And I had corn and hay,
Joe drove the ox, and Tom the swine,
Dick took the foal and mare;
I sold them all- then home to dine,
From famous Banbury fair.

One of the earliest in Cape Breton was the Agricultural Society's fair in Sydney in 1839. The first prize of a cradle scythe went to Alexander Grant of North West Arm for the finest and heaviest bushel of wheat, weighing sixty and a half pounds; and the third prize was won by Michael Mullins of Low Point for the largest crop of potatoes from two measured square rods. The yield averaged five hundred twenty bushels to the acre. (In the early 1990s the average in Nova Scotia was around four hundred bushels).

In 1914 a record potato harvest was made by Thomas Hart of Leitches Creek. From three pounds of Ashley Kidney potato seed, he produced one hundred eighteen pounds of potatoes, and from three pounds of Early Rose he dug one hundred thirty seven pounds. A similar amount of Satisfaction yielded one hundred forty seven and a half pounds. Nine pounds of seed therefore yielded four hundred and two and a half pounds of potatoes.

The first modern local exhibition was held in North Sydney in October, 1909, inside a rink on Blower Street while the animals were in stalls outside. In 1910 the Exhibition moved to Sydney, went back to North Sydney in 1911, and then to Sydney again in 1912 and 1913. The Sydney Exhibition, held on the grounds where the old St Rita's Hospital now stands, was considered to be "the most attractive, best conducted and the most educative agricultural exhibition held in Eastern Canada".

For the rural community Exhibition time is a highlight of summer, preparations beginning the moment the catalogue listing arrives. It can be a frantic time in the farm family, with everyone preparing for a different competition.

All types of livestock are exhibited. Sheep and lambs are groomed; cattle, horses, and even the chickens are washed with Ivory soap, then rinsed and dried, brushed and curried. The stock are hauled to the Exhibition grounds, but not always without incident. One of our ponies, refusing to be loaded, had to be ridden all the way there. Another year sheep escaped while being loaded to return home, leading to a merry chase across the Sydney bypass.

Trunks are packed with gear and special clothing for the horse events. Many people stay over the entire week, and other participants, after doing the morning chores back at the farm, arrive early to do more chores at the Exhibition including the feeding of stock and cleaning of the stables.

Vegetables are displayed. Again, the categories to enter have to be decided upon. The perfect vegetable must be sought and found. Many potatoes are dug to find the required perfect six. And of course there is always "the collection", a category the children in a family try to win year after year, always trying to do better than the year before and to beat the competition. Thorny problems need to be resolved: what does the collection go on - moss or straw? What combinations of vegetables? The result should be like a painting of different colours and textures: smooth green and yellow beans, ruffled cabbage, red tomatoes, orange squashes, red, white and blue potatoes. Sizes and shapes vary: small round radishes, long English cucumbers, frilly cabbages, large pumpkins.

Preparing for the flower sections involves a trip to the fields to look for wildflowers. Then to the garden to search for cuttings for the more formal arrangements, or the perfect gladiola to stand alone.

Then there is "Women's Work", sewing, knitting and such, with the prizes remaining about as unchanged as the name. Women and girls, schedule their baking times and try new recipes and family favorites. Model farms and paintings are created. Prizes are won and trophies and ribbons are hopefully taken home.

There is a saying that "getting there is half the fun", and getting to the Exhibition remains a challenge.

Earlier this century exhibitors from North Sydney travelled on the ferry to Sydney, with boxes of flowers, cartons of bottles and jars, and their livestock. Then they walked from the wharf near the bottom of Dorchester Street to the Exhibition grounds. Activity was frenzied especially when livestock were transported on the ferry or by train and herded along the Esplanade and Kings Road.

On September 4, 1912, using kerosene for fuel and equipped with solid rubber tires, a bus, believed to be the first in Canada, made its maiden run from the centre of Sydney to the Exhibition grounds. Paying five cents each 2,500 passengers rode on the bus that day.

In 1913 the atmosphere was festive with the Fakirs' (Carnival barkers') cries of *"here you are, a dog, a teddy bear and a fountain pen, all for a dime, ten cents, a dime."* Favorite rides were the Merry-go-Round, the Ferris Wheel and the "Ocean Wave", games were toss a hoop over the teddy bears, and hit the bell with a hammer. Swifts Meats had a large roll of back bacon on display and people tried to guess the right weight in ounces. It was all a wonderful opportunity for local politicians to make speeches.

Much has remained the same over the years, although now the pleasure horse events are dominant. The variety and diversity of rural life, demonstrating the self-sufficiency of the people, is no longer there. There were once fish variety competitions, and competitions for the best wooden shingles, leather saddles, flour from Cape Breton wheat, and hand-spun men's knitted underwear.

At the 1936 Exhibition there were still thirty two varieties of apples and twenty seven of plums listed for competition. These are no longer available. Many of the varieties have simply disappeared. However, there is a need to maintain diversity of species. If all diversity is lost, soon all of a species may disappear. The need for high agricultural productivity has meant that we have concentrated on fewer breeds. For example, the Holstein cow is the cow of choice today. It's the best volume producer. But it is bred to specific environmental and feeding conditions and should those conditions alter, the cow has no genetic ability to cope with the additional stress, and breeds which, if crossed with her would produce stronger offspring, may be no longer available. And alternative breeds which could cope may have also disappeared.

We hear of the disappearance of species in the Amazonian rain forest or on the African plains, but some domestic animals and plants may be nearing extinction and are certainly becoming rare. These are animals that people have tended for thousands of years. They are familiar. We depend on them even today for our food.

It has been estimated that by the year 2050 one quarter of the world's plants will be extinct.

There is some hope. Conservancies, like Kew Gardens in London, England, are modern Noah's Arks being established to maintain the genetic vigour of plants and animals.

Besides looking at all the agricultural displays and participating in rides and games, people go to exhibitions to enjoy the food. While long ago fairgoers ate oranges, nuts and gingerbread, today we eat a wider range of foods many of which originated at the St Louis World Fair of 1904.

Workers at that Fair served something called a hamburger. However, a restauranteur claimed his grandfather invented the burger in 1900. He had ground up leftover scraps of raw steak, grilled them, and served the patties on toast from his lunchwagon in downtown New Haven, Connecticut. A group of sailors found his creation similar to a ground beef dish served in Hamburg, Germany, and so called them hamburgers.

The first hot dog was traced to the Polo Grounds in New York in 1894, and to concessionaire Harry Stevens. But a sausage peddlar, Antoine Feuctwanger, at the 1904 Fair, devised the sausage-in-a-bun idea to save on the white gloves he lent to customers so they could hold his hot sausages.

Hot dogs are not always called hot dogs. They can be weiners or frankfurters. Sausages have been made in Germany for centuries. About 1900 an American vendor selling cooked frankfurters, after the sausages made in Franfurt, Germany, called them hot dachshund sausages because they resembled the long bodied dog.

Chips, or French fries, came from France (naturally) about 1870. In England the chipped potatoes teamed up with fried cod, which until then had been served with a slice of bread or a baked potato. Fish and chips made a new complete meal which was enormously successful.

There are conflicting versions of the origin of the ice cream cone. According to one story, at the 1904 Fair Charles Menchez, a salesman, gave a bouquet of flowers and an ice cream and waffle sandwich to his girlfriend. But the bouquet was wet, and so the enterprising girlfriend took one waffle from the sandwich to hold her flowers and wrapped the other into a cone for her ice cream.

Popcorn had become popular much earlier, being introduced by the Indians who brought some to the first American Thanksgiving dinner.

Fall

SEPTEMBER/OCTOBER/NOVEMBER

Come, ye thankful people come,
Raise the song of harvest home;
All is safely gathered in,
Ere the winter storms begin;
God, our Maker, doth provide
For our wants to be supplied;
Come to God's own temple, come,
Raise the song of harvest-home.
"Thanksgiving Hymn" by G.J. Elvey, 1858

SEPTEMBER

September is the seventh month in the old Roman calendar. Other names include Welsh *"Medi" - "the Month of Reaping";* Anglo/Saxon *"Halegmonath" - "the Holy Month";* Celtic *"Witumanoth" - "Wood Month"; "Month of Shedding";* Micmac *"Wikumkewiku's" - "Animal Calling";* and the full moon is the *"Harvest Moon"*, whose light was bright enough for farmers to see by as they continued their harvest.

Thirty days hath September,
April, June and November;
All the rest have thirty-one,
Excepting February alone
And that has twenty-eight days clear
And twenty-nine in each leap year.
Anon.

The falling leaves drift by my window,
The falling leaves of red and gold.
"September Song"

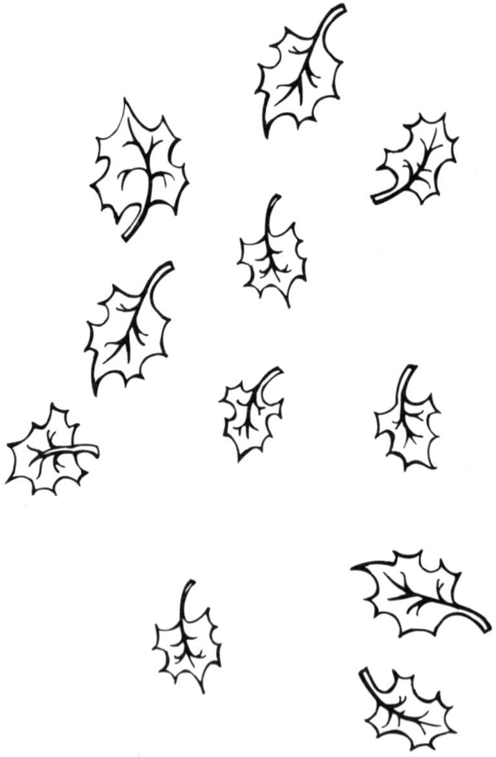

If the weather is fair on September 1 it will continue throughout the month.

"Clear moon, frost soon."

People once believed that bees were as intelligent as human beings. Bees are industrious, wise, "busy", and diligent.

They are associated with death and are symbolic of the soul and of immortality. They are messengers, taking the news of a death to the souls in the next world. Bees are engraved on ancient tombs. (see also end of February) But they are also connected with inspiration and with birth, including that of Zeus, king of the Greek gods. The goddess Demeter was often called the Pure Mother Bee.

Bees needed to be kept informed of events. People told them when there had been a death in the family and when good things like a wedding occured. The hives were then suitably decorated.

Marriage, birth or buryin'
News across the seas,
All your sad or merryin'
You must tell the bees.

"The Bee-boy's Song" by Rudyard Kipling

Years ago, in Britain and parts of North America, the custom was to place in the centre of a hive a small piece of the communion wafer, taken from church. This was called the "little god almighty" and was supposed to protect the bees from all harm and increase their powers of honey making.

There are other superstitions connected with bees. Bees will not thrive if you quarrel with them. Stolen bees will not thrive, but will pine away and die. In England it was considered unlucky to buy or sell bees. They were bartered, for example, for a bushel of corn or a small pig.

Sometimes bees were pursued with the noise from banging on pans and kettles in order to get them to settle down. Alternatively, many people believed the noise might not settle the bees, but it would let the neighbors know there was a swarm in the air.

"You leave them alone/They'll leave you alone."

For a bee sting apply mud, ammonia, or crushed leaves of summer savory. For wasp stings apply mud, a paste of baking soda and water, or use vinegar.

There are a few people in the Maritimes, as well as other places, using bees entirely for their stings. People with multiple schlerosis and arthritis have found that bees, used for their venom, give them more fluid movement and pain has lessened. The venom appears to stimulate the immune system. One treatment involves at least eight stings on specific acupuncture points three times a week.

Honey is used in a variety of ways, from cooking to a spoonful with lemon juice or apple cider vinegar for a "tonic" and as a sugar substitute in tea or coffee. A wide range of colours, consistencies and flavours, from almost white to dark brown, from very sweet to almost bitter, results from the various nectars the bees feed on.

"More Flies are taken with a drop of Honey than a Tun of Vinegar." (Thomas Fuller- 1654-1734- *Gnomologia*)

There were many occasions when neighbours got together to help each other. These were called "bees", an allusion to the social character of the insect. The helping "bees" were preceded by the task at hand such as a spinning bee or a threshing bee.

The women had spinning bees. Anywhere from three to six women or more arrived in the morning carrying their spinning wheels. They stayed all day, spinning most of the household's wool and making a party of it with a good lunch of chicken and vegetables. When finished at the one house, they moved on to another until the neighbourhood wool was spun.

For a barn raising as many as seventy people helped and later there was eating, drinking and dancing.

Entertainment at these bees was similar when neighbours and friends gathered for a visit, or a ceildh as it is known in Gaelic. In the winter stories were told and songs sung. There was always music and dancing to the mouth organ,

bagpipes or fiddles. People danced the shottish or a square set and there was plenty to eat and drink. Elizabeth MacNaughton of St. Patricks Channel summed it up: *"We really enjoyed life to the fullest. We made our own fun. We didn't have much of this world's goods, but we always had plenty to eat."*

Nova Scotia is known for its hospitality. Lieutenant Sleigh, who was stationed at the Sydney garrison in 1846, wrote, *"The hospitality of the farmers and the gentlemen settled in the Province is proverbial, and deserves grateful mention. They have never sent a waggon*(sic) *to market, but some present was forwarded to our cottage. Quarters of lamb, poultry, exquisitely-flavoured butter, vegetables and fruits of every kind, and sundry other produce of the farm-yard, or results of the gun, were daily placed on the larder."*

Today people are still hospitable, going out of their way to make new arrivals feel at home. We were made welcome in a traditional way when we arrived here from New York City. A ceildh was held for us in Little Narrows where our neighbours and those in neighbouring communities of Jubilee and Ottawa Brook presented us with food and other items necessary to help us through our first winter. It was particularly overwhelming to us, having come from a depersonalized city, and we have never forgotten their generosity.

Other gatherings were held, such as Box Socials to raise money for the school. A box, usually bigger than a shoe box, was decorated with tissue paper and ribbons and filled with food to be auctioned. Hopefully a boy would bid on his girlfriend's box. But tricks were played. The auctioneer started the bidding at, say, fifty cents. That was a lot of money in those days but some prankster might increase the bidding to a dollar. One box made local history in Inverness County when a young man, Dan MacKinnon, paid thirty five dollars for sixteen year-old Margaret MacQuarrie's box. He was working in the mines and so, people said, he could afford it; and she was worth it.

During the auction there would be some tense moments, and hearts would be in mouths.

"Going once. Going twice. Going third and last time."

The girl was supposed to sit with the boy who bought her box and dance the first set with him, and later let him take her home, if she liked him.

These socials started before dark when enough people arrived to make a square set. The boxes were auctioned off from llpm to midnight. Eating and dancing continued till dawn when everyone walked home and went to work.

Late in September neighbours went around helping each other with the threshing, which usually took a day. First the grain was tossed on the barn floor where it was threshed, originally by hand, with a thresher made of two sticks about a yard long and about an inch and a half around. These were tied together by a longer string, rope or wire. When swung over the shoulder and down to hit the stalks on the barn floor, the oat or barley seed separated from the stalk. The grain was scooped up and put into a wecht, also known as a fanner. This was made of thin wood bent in a circle and covered with animal skin. Holes were randomly pierced through the skin with a hot iron. The grain was tossed in the wecht and any remaining chaff blew away.

Before the use of motors a big treadmill and a set of fanners were set up on the barn floor. Workhorses were put on the treadmill and a halter was hitched to the bar that went across. The horses stayed in the same place and kept up a slow steady walk. Two men up in the scaffolding fed the oats to the fanners. The chaff flew all over the barn. Children were given a little dish or an empty lard pail to collect the oats and put them in barrels or boxes for winter feed.

The threshing machine replaced the hand flail. Basically it was a wooden box containing a wooden cylinder with iron spikes projecting around the outside which, when rotated, struck the grain and separated the grain from the head of the stalk.

A treadmill provided power. Treadmills of this type consisted of a chute mounted on an inclined platform and operated on the principle of an endless belt. The weight of the horse trying to walk uphill supplied the power.

Ingenuity and a creative imagination went into the early inventions of farm equipment. At the Paris Exhibition of 1855 various new threshing machines were exhibited. And *"during the operation, to ascertain the comparative rapidity and economy of threshing, six men were engaged in threshing with flails, who, in one hour, threshed sixty litres of wheat. In the same time*

Pitt's American machine threshed 740 litres

Clayton's English " " 410 "

Duvoir's French " " 250 "

Pinet's " " " 150 " "

A French journal, speaking of this trial, said, *"This American machine literally devoured the sheaves of wheat. The eye cannot follow the work which is effected between the entrance of the sheaves, and the end of the operation. It is one of the greatest results which it is possible to obtain. The impression which the spectacle produced...was profound." (THE FARMERS BOOK OF PRACTICAL INFORMATION* - Dickerman. 1880)

In fall winter's food is stored and seed for the next spring's planting is set aside. Seeds were gathered in fair weather (often at the wane of the moon), cleaned, sorted and put in wood boxes, barrels, leather bags or earthenware vessels. Kidney type beans were shelled, dried and sometimes kept upstairs in a corner of the hall in a flour barrel covered with a "petticoat" of cotton material.

Jars of preserves, pickles and vegetables were literally "put down" in the root cellar for storage. Here the earth floor, stone walls without central heating, provided a perfect storage area as the cellar kept foods cool in summer and above freezing in winter. Potatoes, apples and carrots, stored in sawdust, would last until the following spring. Cellar is the mispronounced French word cella - storeroom. Cellars were not always under the house. Sometimes they were placed outside, off to one side, usually the north side.

Blueberries, cranberries and other small fruits were dried, mixed with meat and stuffed, sausage like, into an intestine casing.

Today we still "can" a few things, but for the most part these are relishes, chutneys and pickles, while meats, fish and vegetables are more easily put down in the freezer.

Dried beans were a popular staple. Two cups of dried beans, along with a pork scrap for flavour, were used for the traditional pot of beans every Wednesday and Saturday. All the salt was removed from the pork by wiping it with a cloth. Then the meat was diced, keeping the rind on, put in the bottom of a pot with enough water to float the beans.

Salt, pepper and a little mustard were added and the mixture was cooked all day. Another favorite meal was fried potatoes, beans and turnips.

Cape Breton's first major farming settlement was established in the early 1700's by Louis-Simon Le Poupet, the Sieur of Boularderie, at his concessions along the little Bras d'Or (the island now bears his name - Boularderie). He had high hopes of growing sufficient produce to feed the occupants of Louisbourg Fortress and to supply them with coal and wood.

He built houses, a good road, a large storehouse, a saw mill and a flour mill. His son arrived to help him in 1737, only to find the property rights were not clear and there were numerous debts.

Within a few years he was growing wheat and a large garden and orchard, alongside a dairy, stable, dovecote, wind mill and a water mill that ground his corn. There were problems as men brought over to farm found that fishing was more lucrative and they had to be compelled to work the land. Boularderie also started a shipbuilding enterprise, and had flakes for drying fish and a storehouse for salt used in salting fish. Wheat was ground for flour and bread made from it for the people at the Fortress. In 1745 when New Englanders attacked the Fortress, Boularderie was wounded, taken prisoner and his property destroyed.

Most early settlers' homesteads were small. At first only potatoes were grown. Later these were followed by small crops of oats, wheat, turnips and Indian corn. Hay was stored in a log barn. Crops were protected by bristling rows of stakes known as a "dog leg fence". Calves were tethered near the house and the cows allowed to pasture in the woods.

In 1796, Captain Cox, of the Sydney Garrison, was granted a large parcel of land along Spanish River (now Sydney River), which he cleared with the help of his soldiers, military duties being light. He built a house, outbuildings, a grist mill and a lime kiln to handle the limestone, which was quarried nearby and used as fertilizer. Coxheath, as his property became known, has good agricultural land and continued to be a major farming area, supplying the growing population of Sydney and surrounding areas, especially after the construction of the steel plant at the turn of this century. Today, however, the area is a built up suburb and although many homes have their own vegetable plots, few farms remain.

The first recorded export of agricultural products from Cape Breton was a shipment of potatoes from Sydney to

Halifax in 1796. The following year more potatoes, along with eighty four sheep, were shipped to Newfoundland, (St. John's, Burin, Fortune Bay and Placentia). Exports were mainly on locally made shallops and schooners, thus increasing the profits to the island.

By 1829 exports included potatoes, oats and barley, cattle, sheep, swine, horses, butter, cheese, salt beef and pork, and plums. Wheat went to Halifax, oats and potatoes to the West Indies, butter, eggs, oats and potatoes to St. Pierre and Miquelon. Chief ports of export were Baddeck, Great Bras d'Or, Port Hood, Bridgeport, Margaree, St. Anns, North Sydney, Arichat and Sydney. Cattle came down to Sydney on ferries as well as on scows, powered by two sets of oars and a sail.

Agriculture began to decline at the end of the nineteenth century as many young people left farms for the promise of an easier life and more money. The coal mines and the steel and iron works acted as a magnet. And transportation was now easier. The railroad came in 1891 and there continued to be a network of ferries working the waterways of the island, such as around the Bras d'Or, down North and to other places. In the 1890's the Plant Line, one of several which had sailings from Cape Breton, ran weekly trips, ice and weather permitting, to Boston and back. In 1931 Canadian National ran three round trips weekly to Boston from Sydney. Travel between Cape Breton and "the Boston States" was common and there were cases of people who had been to Boston but not to Baddeck.

In two years alone (1926 & 1927), over eight thousand Cape Bretoners left the island, having obtained papers at the U.S. consulate at Sydney. In addition there were many others who went to Halifax, Central or Western Canada, or the United States from other ports.

Produce has always been brought from the farms into the more populated areas. It was written in the early 1800's, *"Between Sydney Forks and St Peters there wasn't a cart to be seen except one owned by a man named Howie. The people used to bring their produce on drags - a pair of poles, one end hung each side of the horse and the other end trailing on the ground. They would leave these poles in town for firewood and ride home on horseback. Their harness was made of straw, and I've seen a cow eat the harness of a horse in the street here* (Sydney). *The garrison made a good market and spent a good deal of money."*

Farm produce continued to be brought into the towns, first by horse and wagon, later by truck. And when the boom started in Sydney in the early 1900's, local farmers could not produce enough food. It is ironic that the development of industry created a greater demand for produce which gave more revenue to the farmer, but at the same time attracted the farmers' offspring to the city. This resulted in the eventual decline of the farming industry and many fields reverted to the trees which had been, a generation or so earlier, so laboriously cleared.

OCTOBER

October is the eighth month of the Roman Calendar.

Other names include Welsh *"Hydref"* - *"the month of autumn"*; Gaelic "An *Damhair"* - *"the month of deer rutting"*; Anglo/Saxon *"Wintirfyllith"* - *"month of the winter moon"*; Saxon *"Wyn moneth"* - *"Wine Month"*; *"Winter fyllith"* from the approach of winter with the full moon of the month; and Micmac *"Wikewiku's"* - *"animals fat"*. The full moon is known as *"Hunter's Moon"*.

"All the plenty summer pours;
Autumn's rich o'erflowing stores;
Flocks that whiten all the plain;
Yellow sheaves of ripened grain..."
by C. Kocer, 1838

Some advice for the fall is that one should avoid being out late at nights or in foggy weather; for if a person gets a cold now, he will have it all winter.

This month hot drinks and meals be good
To keep thy health and nourish thy blood
Provide warm clothes, and go foot-dry
Thou shalt escape much danger thereby.

Anon.

Indian Summer, with its warm and mild weather in the middle of cooler autumn, is a reminder of summer. All too soon though there are signs of winter.

It is still said that when the leaves do not fall from the trees in October, or when there are a great number of caterpillars on the trees, a cold winter is coming. If the birds are fat in October, expect a hard winter. If an onion skin is thick or if wasps build their nests high off the ground, we will have a cold, snowy winter.

Icy weather in October presages a mild Christmas or vice versa.

If ducks do slide at Halloweentide
At Christmas they will swim.
If ducks do swim at Halloweentide
At Christmas they will slide.

Horses and cattle begin to get their shaggy heavy coats as an added protection against the cold weather. And, before winter "officially" arrives, the brooks will fill up three times, from three heavy rainstorms.

If Christmas comes during a waxing, increasing, moon there will be a good year ahead. The nearer Christmas to the new moon, the better the next year will be. If Christmas comes during a waning or decreasing moon, there will be a hard year ahead.

The cranberry harvest marked the end of the harvest season. A good picker, using a wooden scoop, like a big dust-pan with a high back and tines like a big comb, could pick ("scoop") one hundred pounds an hour. The bog was flooded and berries scooped from the water. Today mechanical harvesters do the job commercially, but there are still many individuals who scoop by hand.

Cranberries got their name from cranes that lived in the bogs and ate the berries from the plant which had pink blossoms that looked like the heads of the cranes. The berries are also called bounce berries, because their ripeness is tested by their ability to bounce rather than by size or color. Children once played a game in which each person was given seven chances to bounce berries over a four inch high hurdle.

Cranberries are rich in vitamins A and C, iodine and calcium. They were stored dried or sailors would store them raw in barrels of fresh water. Unlike the British sailors who were called Limeys because they ate limes, also a source of vitamin C against scurvy, North American sailors, who ate cranberries, were not called Crannies.

Cranberry juice is used in the treatment of urinary tract infections or the treatment of kidney stone problems and even in helping cure diaper rash. It remains a popular beverage and today there is a wide variety of combinations available with other fruit juices. The bright red juice can also be used as a dye for rugs, blankets and cloth.

Indians used cranberries to draw the poison from arrow wounds. Or they dried them, crushed and mixed them with dried venison and fat drippings, to make pemmican. Shaped into little cakes and baked in the sun, they lasted.

Early settlers in New England and Nova Scotia made cranberry soap and cranberry candles. Berries are also mixed with other ingredients for relish and with whisky for a drink called "American BiCentennial", also known as a "fire-cracker". The first commercial can of berries was packed in 1912 in Massachusetts.

Although butchering took place throughout the year the main season was the fall, when the weather turned cold and the animals were fat from summer pasture. Most communities had a neighbourhood butcher who, with the help of the farmer, would do the slaughtering. Pigs were fattened for six weeks with extra feed and apples, which gave the meat a good flavour. There were often neighbourhood competitions to see who had the fattest pig.

A pig is intelligent and it has been said that a dog looks up to you, a cat down at you, but a pig looks you in the eye as an equal. Every part of a pig can be used except for his squeal.

Bacon and hams are made by curing the meat and good homemade lard comes from rendering back fat and trimmings. Sometimes a hole was dug outside and lined with tin. Then the ham was wrapped in cheescloth and a flour or sugar bag, put in a box, lowered into the hole and covered with earth. The ham was taken out the following Easter.

Pigskins are used for gloves, footballs and in the treatment of burns.

Many animals though were sold alive to butchers from town, like Jack MacDonald of Sydney and his father before him. Jack scoured the countryside looking for animals. Once he had located them the farmer was usually responsible for getting the stock to the train or the ferry for transport to Sydney. Here it was met and driven through the streets to the MacDonald slaugterhouse on the Esplanade at Townsend Street. Sometimes the animals were cooperative, while other times they escaped and raced around town. Jack had a ram trained to help him control the lambs.

Later, butchers took larger trucks to pick up animals at the source of sale. Jack travelled in all types of weather and was known for paying cash up front. Loading animals on his truck was usually a challenge, with much heaving, pushing and chasing, and some got loose.

Jack also bought wool after shearing, and hides throughout the year. For some farmers the sale of stock paid their yearly taxes.

More recently many farmers ship their stock to the weekly auctions in Truro.

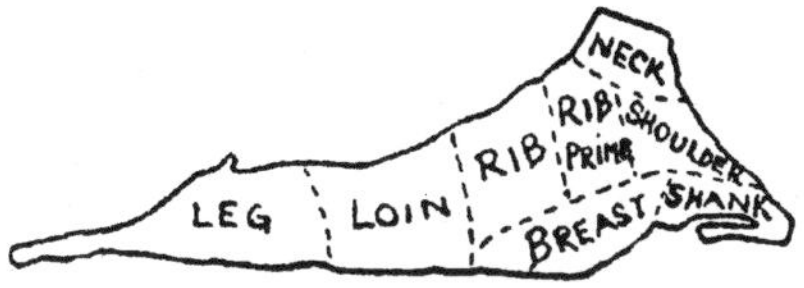

A SIDE OF MUTTON

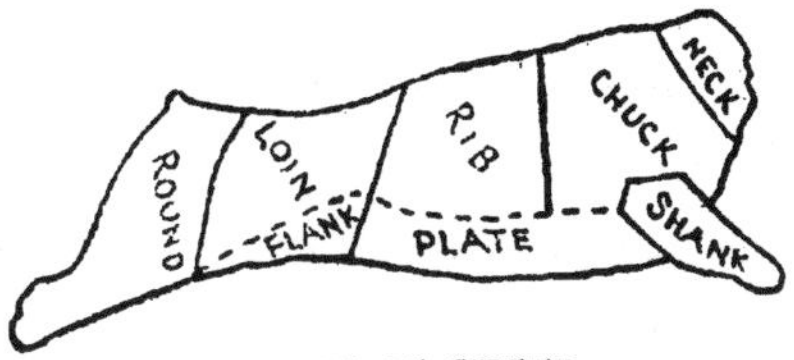

A SIDE OF SHEEP

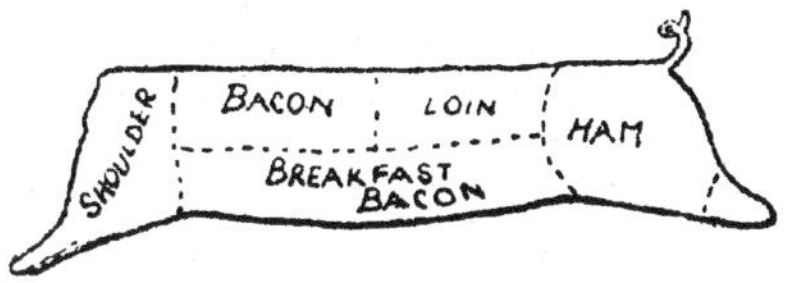

A SIDE OF PORK

There are different ways of preserving meat, and this was particularly important before the use of refrigeration. Curing preserves the meat and gives it added flavour. To tenderize it beef was hung in a barn, milkhouse or other cool place and left for at least ten days. Beef was wrapped in muslin or cloth and it would hopefully last the winter in a cold place.

Lambs were butchered as needed. A lamb would be divided between a few neighbours, then the next week, another neighbour would butcher one of his lambs and divide that meat.

Originally mincemeat was a mixture of finely chopped or minced meat, suet, fresh and dried fruits, and nuts, citron, molasses, sugar, spices and brandy and other spirits or cider. Today, the meat and suet are frequently left out, leaving a mixture of fruits, spices and sweeteners. A mock mincemeat is also made using green tomatoes instead of meat. Mincemeat is a particularly old and traditional harvest food, today used primarily at Thanksgiving and Christmas.

Portions of venison, rabbit, beef or veal, as well as the delicate meat of tongues of deer, calves, cattle are still turned into specialties.

Women made different kinds of "puddings". A white pudding had flour, rolled oats, minced onions, cut or shredded suet, and salt and pepper. These were mixed and put into hog casings (intestines), tied at both ends and boiled until done. Then they were dried and stored in the kitchen loft. Black or blood puddings were made the same way but with the addition of blood, gathered from the hog at butchering. Sheep's intestines were used as casings for sausages.

Potted head or headcheese was easily made. The pig's head was put in a pot, covered with water and simmered until the meat fell off. This was ground and mixed with some broth and gelatine added, as well as onions, salt, pepper and summer savory, and stored in casings or molds.

One method of preserving fish, meats or poultry is by smoking. After curing, the meat is hung in the smokehouse which may be as small as a barrel but is usually larger. Dried apple wood, hickory, maple, ash, oak and dry willow are the best woods for smoking, giving a slow, smouldering fire. Sawdust and corncobs have also been used. Smoking gives the meat an extra flavour but has recently fallen out of favour.

Waste lard, fat from cooking, and fats rendered from tallow and meat trimmings made soap, while candles came from the fat of sheep or cows.

The fall was also the season for preparing wool for knitting or weaving. Earlier the shorn wool had been divided. The household needs were considered and enough wool for mitts, socks, sweaters, men's underwear, bloomers and leg warmers was set aside. Some winter underwear, as well as blankets and material, was woven on looms. The rest of the wool was either shipped to the larger woolen mills, like Stanfields in Truro or Condons Mills in Prince Edward Island, or was packed into a wagon and taken to a local mill, like Glendyer Mills in Inverness County. Farm women often preferred to get blankets in return instead of cash. They also exchanged the raw wool at the mills for soft flannel that they could make into undershirts, while other material was used for underdrawers for the men, pants, stockings, and dresses (Glendyer Mills had a lovely heather color material for dresses). Although women made many articles of clothing, there was usually a tailor in the neighbourhood as well.

Wool still is often dyed in a wide range of colours by using plants from the garden or fields. The natural wool itself added to the colour range, with each breed of sheep having a different shade.

A rusty red can be produced using dahlia flowers, and shades of pink come from crabapples.

Blues come from elderberries, blackberries, blueberries, iris flowers, or indigo, and a purple may be made by boiling rusty nails or other iron in vinegar with some alum.

Yellow sources are numerous: the blossoms of marigolds, chrysanthemums, zinnias, dandelions, daylilies, goldenrod, and Queen Anne's Lace. Tumeric, saffron, onion skins and urine are also used.

For greens, blue lupines are steeped in lime water and nitrate of copper, or the stems, canes and leaves of Floribunda roses, spinach leaves and seaweed.

Browns come from lichen or moss from off rocks, white birchbark, yellow dock, acorns, beets, Queen Anne's Lace, red onion skins, coffee or tea, seaweed, sunflower seeds, dried tomato vines and pine cones.

Wood charcoal gives a range of grays to black.

The early settlers also raised flax which was then turned into linen.

During hard times even flour and sugar bags were used to make clothing. The sheep, it was said, "took care of the clothing" and provided a blanket as well. And the selling of "the cattle took care of the boots".

There was little or no waste and every scrap of material was used. Strips of old cloth and yarn from old sweaters were recycled into braided rugs which could be artistic as well as functional.

A sign of fall is the smell of burning leaves although this practice is frowned on by those who consider that the leaves should be composted. Years ago there were other uses for the fallen leaves which were gathered and stuffed into covers to make matresses.

Feathers also were used to stuff mattresses and pillows. Ducks and geese were plucked with even the wing and tail feathers, although not as soft, being used.

There is good fishing in the fall. Mackerel runs last about two weeks and the fish still are salted in barrels. Fish will only absorb so much salt and a brine forms, preserving the mackerel for the winter.

Fall salmon runs begin when the leaves turn. This depends on the weather for the leaves do not turn when it is warm.

Indians moved inland in the Fall to catch eel, salmon and other migratory fish and surplus fish and deer meat were often traded for tea, sugar and potatoes.

Fall is also hunting season.

Supplying the early settlers with meat would not have depleted the large herds in northern Cape Breton, but the demand for hides did. Moose hides fetched ten shillings a piece and in the winter of 1789-90 hunters flocked to Cape Breton to make a killing in more than one way.

Before that winter had ended more than nine thousand moose carcasses were left rotting and the stench pervaded the air for miles. Passing ships' captains and crews complained about the foul smell coming from Cape Breton. Led by guides, an expedition of officers and thirty men of the 21st Regiment set out from the garrison at Sydney on snowshoes and toboggans and carrying copies of the ordinance passed by council on Dec 21, 1789, to stop the poachers.

Today moose are not plentiful and there have been years when the population has been so low that all hunting of them has been banned.

Once caribou were plentiful. They could co-exist with moose. Indians, French at Louisbourg, soldiers at the garrison in Sydney, and settlers hunted them. Ships were supplied with their meat and fishermen depended on caribou for their winter supply. Caribou were easy to hunt and kill. The 1898 Nova Scotia Game Laws stated that "No person shall kill more than two moose and two caribou". Although there was an abudance of caribou, by the end of the nineteenth century, virtually all caribou had disappeared from Cape Breton, except for a few remaining in the Highlands.

Their decline benefitted the white tailed deer who were beginning to return to Cape Breton. Deer were abundant in Nova Scotia until about the year 1200 when the colder winters with deep snow caused them to disappear. Caribou then surplanted deer. Now the deer were returning.

The beginning of this century was remarkable. Deer became so common that in 1922 an open season was declared in Richmond County. It lasted until 1928, when all Cape Breton was opened. Deer were not officially reported as being in the Highlands National Park until 1924 and the years from 1944 to 1956 were "golden years" for the deer hunter.

Today many men leave their city jobs to return to the woods at hunting season. Most hunters are serious about their sport. They appreciate being part of the natural environment, while a few simply want to get away from the city with "the boys".

Years ago hunting was an essential part of survival. Indian hunters often spent four or five days seeking game and returned for help in hauling out the kill, which would be split among families. Now the Indian communities are larger, but a good catch of deer or fish is still shared with family and friends.

Caribou meat is something like corned beef. Sometimes small pieces were put on a stick and roasted over a fire. Other times pieces were attached to a cord and hung between two poles over a fire. The cord was twisted and then released. The meat cooked as it turned. It could also be boiled in a "kettle" hollowed out of a large log, or a metal pot. Rocks, hot from the fire, were dropped into the kettle to heat the water. Cooled rocks were removed and other heated rocks added until the meat was cooked. Berries or leaves were added for seasoning.

We no longer throw hot rocks into kettles. Instead we have barbeques in our backyards and it is more likely to be hamburgers or lamb or beef kebobs with vegetables on a skewer than caribou or moose. Hot dogs on a stick and roasted over an open campfire still remains a special summertime treat.

In the fall birds such as partridges are hunted. A seven pound partridge can be stuffed and roasted, but anything from two to four pounds is too small and may be stewed instead.

The Indians hunted birds at night. They carried unlit torches with them, lay in the canoes and allowed them to drift among the sleeping birds. The torches were lit, surprising the birds who flew confused into the air and around the lights, where they were knocked down with sticks.

Today it is illegal to hunt with lights although sometimes people are caught "jacking" deer by using flashlights. Unlike birds, deer are mesmerized by lights and stand still.

October is pumpkin month. They are used for Jack o'Lanterns as well as in pies. In North America we use pumpkins but in old Scotland, where there were no pumpkins, children at Halloween used large turnips, hollowed out, with carved faces and candles inside. Called "baygies" or turnip lanterns, they were hung or carried to scare witches. Irish children used turnips or potatoes and in parts of England large beets (punkies) were used.

It was once believed that Jack o'Lanterns were the souls of sinners condemned to walk the earth until the end of time. One such sinner was an Irishman named Jack. Too wicked for heaven he was also expelled from hell for playing tricks on the devil. The devil threw him a chunk of live coal which Jack put in the turnip he was eating. Jack has been wandering the earth ever since. This is an echo of the fires and torches of ancient Halloween celebrations and of the Celtic festival of the dead, linking people with dead souls who wander the earth at that time. Readers may remember that a broken pumpkin was all that was left of Ichabod Crane, the superstitious schoolmaster of Sleepy Hollow in early New York.

Pumpkins are also used in cooking pies, preserves, soup, puddings, muffins and loaves.

Recently, Nova Scotia has become famous for giant pumpkins. Howard Dill of Windsor began growing giant pumpkins in the Sixties and soon achieved international recognition. Raising these giants for competition is a growing "sport" and Howard Dill's pumpkin seed is sold all over the world. Today a few of these giant pumpkins weigh in at over one thousand pounds.

Festivals marking the end of the harvesting are still celebrated with feasting at Thanksgiving. There are services, followed by a supper, and churches are decorated with fruits, flowers and produce.

The ancient Mayas had a yearly pilgrimage to their holy city where they gave thanks to the god of the harvest for their corn. He was a handsome young god, symbolizing life and growth, and his head was covered with corn rather than hair. These Mayas added an extra festivity. Along with their feasting they also watched ballgames which were accompanied by the music of trumpets and drums.

Thanksgiving is still associated with sports, especially football.

Thanksgiving is usually pictured as a traditional New England Thanksgiving, complete with turkey dinner and trimmings. But the practice of setting aside a special day of thanksgiving did not originate in New England. There were days set aside to give thanks that there had been no earthquakes or devastating hurricanes. England had a day to celebrate the defeat of the Spanish Armada.

The first Thanksgiving in North America was celebrated in May, 1578, by the English settlers to Newfoundland with a simple church service.

American Thanksgiving commemorates the first harvest of the Pilgrims and it is now a general Thanksgiving for the blessings of the year. In November, 1621, the Pilgrims held a day of prayer and a feast which lasted for three days. In addition to the wild turkeys, cranberries and pumpkin, the Indians brought deer to eat along with fish, eels, clams and oysters, corn bread and roasted corn, and a pudding of corn and molasses.

Throughout the years, the food has varied little. The wealthy might have had a turkey at one end of the table and a chicken pie at the other and a possible side dish of pigeon pie. Well-to-do farm households had a smaller turkey and no pie, while poorer farmers had a pie but no turkey. Everyone had cider and mince pie.

A few Thanksgiving customs have disappeared. Turkey raffles of leftover birds were once held at the end of Thanksgiving eve. Special shooting matches were also held in the morning. A baseline was marked in an open field. From this line different shooting distances were laid down. For example, eight rods was "chicken distance", nine rods a "turkey distance". Turkeys were targets as well as prizes. These matches were not viewed favourably by the church since they kept too many away from morning service.

Thanksgiving was celebrated, but it had no specific date in the States until 1863 when President Lincoln set aside a day for the entire nation. This continues to be the last Thursday of November.

Canada's celebrations are different. In 1763, Halifax had a day of Thanksgiving for the conclusion of the Peace of Paris, which gave Canada to Britain. In Upper Canada, Thanksgiving was observed on June 18, 1816, in thanks for the end of the war between Great Britain and Napoleon.

After Confederation, the first Thanksgiving proclamation was issued March 1, 1871 in thanks for the restoration of the health of the Prince of Wales.

The first Thanksgiving as we now know it was observed November 6, 1879. Since then it has been proclaimed annually. For a time the date was the same as that in the United States, but it was found to be too late in the year for Canadians and too near Christmas.

The date was changed to October and generally set for a Thursday. After the First World War, Thanksgiving was proclaimed for the week in which Armistice Day occurred. Thanksgiving Day and Armistice Day were then merged and celebrated under the name of Armistice Day on November 11, the day the First World War ended.

In 1931, the act that had established Armistice Day was amended and the name of the holiday changed to Remembrance Day. Thanksgiving Day again was proclaimed as an October holiday. Since 1957 Thanksgiving has been the second Monday in October.

At about this time houses were "banked" against winter winds. The banking covered the sills at the base of the house to prevent drafts. A bank was made of a wide layer of sawdust, wood chips, seaweed or eel grass. Eel grass, abundant around the coastline, was a nuisance to fishermen as it clogged nets and fouled boat propellers. But it made a decent banking material. Manure was used to bank the sill of the barn. Banking was taken down again in the spring so that sills did not rot.

NOVEMBER

November is the ninth month of the Roman calendar. Other names inlude Welsh *"Tachwedd"* - *"the Month of Slaughtering"* or *"Y Mis Du"* - *"the Black Month"*; Anglo/Saxon *"Blotmonath"* -*"the Month of Blood"*; Micmac *"Keptiku's"* - *"Frozen Water"*. The full moon was the *"Fog"* or *"Beaver Moon"*.

November's sky is chill and drear,
November's leaf is red and sear.
"Marmion" by Sir Walter Scott

How well I know what I mean to do
When the long, dark autumn-evenings come -
"By the Fireside" by Robert Browning

Now, after hunting and butchering, hides are turned into leather. Indians often softened hides by rubbing animal parts and oil on them to make them supple. The hides were then smoked to help preserve them and to add colour.

Other hides were scraped, cleaned and laid, hair side down, to be cured on a layer of salt. More coarse salt was sprinkled on top of the hide. Layers of hides and salt were built up and, if placed on a sloping floor, the brine could drain. Cow hides were cured in about two weeks while sheepskins only took four or five days to be ready for tanning, shipping and further processing.

Sewing needles made of bone and thread from animal tendons made the Indians' clothing, which might also be decorated with intricate patterns of porcupine quills. Moccasins and leggings were made from hides. The sole of the moccasin came from the heavier part of the hide near the backbone. Inch-wide straps from the backbone hide of mink were the most valuable because this part was thicker and stronger. Calfskin hides were finer and used to make laces for women's shoes. Leggings, or larrigans, were made from well oiled leather. There were different styles: one had a moccasin bottom, stovepipe legging and tongue, and was laced up the front; another had the mocassin bottom, the stovepipe legging and a single lace through belt-like loops to draw the top closed above the calf.

Hides were also used for harnesses.

During the First World War hides were in demand. Money received for a hide paid for the animal, and the meat was profit.

Stocking up supplies for the winter is one sign of its approach and another sign is the migration of birds to the warm south. Especially visible is the V made by migrating geese.

Another sign is the arrival by mail of the "Wish Book", the Christmas catalogue from Sears or other mail order houses, and many hours are spent intensely studying all the wonderful things they contain.

In winter the arrival of seed catalogues is a sign of spring. They offer glimpses into the next growing season and give the senses pleasure in planning and remembering past summers' gardens.

Also at this time the almanacks for the coming year appear. These continue to be sources of interesting facts about the moon, fixed and moveable feasts, calendar notes, agricultural tips (hints on ploughing, insect control, planting, the best time to dig potatoes), household hints, advertisements, and civic information.

Farming began to change in the middle of the 1800s. Farmers were advised to learn more about their business and encouraged to take pride in using modern agricultural practices. Belcher's FARMER'S ALMANACK of 1878 even went so far as to state that *"It is the duty of every farmer in the Province (of Nova Scotia) to visit the Annual Agricultural Exhibition, and to take his family with him, in order that they may realize the advances that are being made in the culture of the soil, and the improvement of farm animals."*

In 1882 they were advised that *"Nova Scotia Agriculture has entered upon an entirely new phase. Our Agriculturalists are, in many districts, zealously seeking after scientific methods of culture, introducing labour saving machinery, and improving their livestock."*

Earlier, in 1847, agriculture had taken on a philosophical and religious fervour. The Governor General, the Earl of Elgin, speaking to gathered farmers said *"What does the promotion of agricultural improvement in Canada involve? I need not remind you that in all countries, and in all conditions of society, agriculture ranks high as an honorable useful pursuit...*

"Agriculture as a science is rapidly becoming more important, and attracting the attention of many persons. It is the noblest, for it is the natural employment of man - the intelligent and independent farmer is ever requested; he holds an important and responsible place in society...

"Men must be educated to be farmers, as well as lawyers, doctors or divines. And there are many young men in stores and offices, who ought to be engaged in agricultural pursuits - it would be better for them, and for the province at large - and who among the number would not rather be an independent farmer than a petty shopkeeper, or a fourth rate lawyer."

Milling frolics, still held here in Cape Breton, were part of the community preparations for winter. Neighbours go from house to house preparing woven cloth, making it supple and soft, so that it can be turned into finished products. The milling board, with grooves, is set up, usually in the kitchen, with room for about twelve people along each side. The frolic starts early in the evening, and when one group has finished a turn another takes its place. The long single strip of cloth, just off the loom, is soaked in warm water and oatmeal, then wrung enough to keep water from dripping.

It takes from three to five hours to "mill" about thirty yards of homespun for trousers and jackets. This requires much pounding. Blankets take less time.

When milling the cloth is stretched out, grabbed tightly, rubbed, turned, pounded and passed along. This brings the nap (the soft, downy surface) out of the material and shrinks it. The combination of movements is accompanied by singing, on Cape Breton, in Gaelic, following the tradition of their ancestors. A "lunch" is prepared: in the early days this would consist of herring and blue potatoes, or baked beans and brown bread, but always biscuits or bannock, and tea.

Another method of preparation was to stretch the cloth after it had been in water, *"in a tenting field, long stakes set closely with small, angled iron hooks. The stakes were secured to the tops of high poles crossing the field like a fence. One selvedge of the wet cloth was stretched evenly along the top hooks; the lower selvedge was then pulled down and secured on a lower set of tenting hooks, driven into a heavy lower bar. This bar, swinging on the cloth, pulled it down 'full width'. The cloth was then left to dry taut and tight - upon 'tenter hooks'. In some old pieces of English flannel you can still see along the selvedge the marks of tenter hooks."* The expression remains today. People who are nervous, anxious and tense are said to be "on tenterhooks". The words tense and tension also are derived from the "stretched out" Latin word "tensus".

November 30, St. Andrew's Day is celebrated by Scots everywhere. Kilts are put on, haggis toasted and, as later on his birthday, Robert Burns' songs are sung. St. Andrew, the patron saint of Scotland, was Christ's first disciple. His Day marks the beginning of Advent, the four week period of preparation heralding the birth of Christ, and the first festival of the Christian year.

Winter

December/January/February

The north wind doth blow,
And we shall have snow
And what will poor Robin do then?
Poor thing.
He'll sit in a barn,
And keep himself warm,
And hide his head under his wing
Poor thing.

DECEMBER

December is the tenth month of the Roman Calendar. Other names include Welsh, "Rhagfyr" - "the Month of Preparation"; Gaelic, "An Mios marbh" - "the Dead Month"; Anglo/Saxon, "Giuli" - "the Month of Yule"; Micmac "Keptiku's" - "Frozen Water"; Celtic, "Heilagamanoth" - "Holy Month". The full moon is the "Wolf Moon" or the "Cold Moon".

The night has a thousand eyes,
And the day but one;
Yet the light of the bright world dies
With the dying sun.
"Light" by Francis W. Bourdillon

And after him came next the chill December;
Yet he through merry feasting which he made,
And great bonfires, did not the cold remember...
And in his hand a broad deepe bowle he beares,
Of which he freely drinks an health to all his peeres.
by Edmund Spenser

People conditioned themselves for the winter - so do animals.

Cattle and horses grow thicker coats and the wool on sheep has grown back by this time.

Codfish are thicker and fatter in December.

Cod for the winter was salted in bulk. Placed flat with the first layer of fish belly up, salt was added; then a layer with the back up was salted, next a layer belly up, and so on until the stack was about three feet high. This supply lasted all winter.

It was essential to also have a supply of meat. Often there was not enough food to carry the livestock through the winter and so the herds were culled, some being sold, some butchered.

Hunting was also necessary. In primitive socities, rituals preceded the hunt. Usually conducted by a shaman or medicine man. This most important member of the tribe was also a spiritual guide, a teacher, an interpreter of mysteries. He used sound, music, dance and masks in his work. Dressed in animal skins, wearing horns on his head, and so disguised as the animals or something else in nature, he entered a trance state and became one with them. (see also Valentine's Day)

Masks have various meanings and hide the true identity of the person wearing them. This allows that person to either change places with the creature represented by the mask, or to actually become one with it. A mask can also hide a person from Death. If he is pretending to be someone or something else, Death may not find him.

Today, masks and disguises are worn at Halloween, an eerie time of year when it is said the dead walk the earth, and at the winter holiday season with mummering and carnivals much is done to excess. We eat too much, drink too much, party too much, spend too much money. Many seem to follow the philosophy of to eat, drink and be merry, for tomorrow we die.

When we disguise ourselves, abandoning our normal behaviour, it may be that we subconsciously inherit the ways of our forefathers and, like them, are seeking to avoid death.

December 21 is the Winter Solstice, the shortest day and the longest night, and it is a great turning point of the year. There have always been elaborate celebrations by every civilization at this time, when it was particularly important to worship the sun since its power was depleted.

The sun gives warmth and energy but it also has a destructive side.

In order to explain the mysteries of life man invented myths. Gods and demigods emerged and brought some understanding of the chaos.

At the Winter Solstice the ancient Hindus, Persians and Romans celebrated the birth of Mithra, their sun god, the "undying, shining, swift-horsed Sun". The Romans called the Winter Solstice day Dies Natalis Invicti Solis, "the Birthday of the Unconquered Sun", the god Mithra who, as an embodiment of Light, rode a fiery chariot across the sky.

The Celts and other peoples associated horses with the sun. Their speed and prestige carry the sky god into battle. In many myths the sun was carried across the sky in a chariot pulled by horses. Ancient Chinese myths have the sun god driving a chariot pulled by a dragon-horse. The ancient Egyptian barge of the sun disappears behind the western mountain on its nocturnal path towards the east and the return of day. This voyage by the sun god Ra also figures in the Egyptian Books of the Dead as a symbol of the soul's journey through the underworld toward rebirth. In Greece the arrival of the reborn light is depicted in the ascension of the Greek sun god Helios. He charges up the sky in his solar chariot drawn by a team of fiery horses.

Celebrations of the Winter Solstice have come down to us as confused memories. Today we celebrate the Solstice, but we call it the holiday season. Customs, modified by time, remain.

From the middle to the end of December, the ancient Romans honoured Saturn, god of Agriculture. His name derives from sator (a sower) or with satur (stuffed or gorged). He was usually depicted with a sickle or with ears of corn. He was also connected with Cronus, the father of time and fertlility and was himself identified as Father Time. As late as the fourteenth century he is pictured sitting holding his wheel, symbol of the sun and also the cycle of the year, and a child, representing the new year, on his lap. Today, Father Time is shown as a slender old man dressed in a monk's robe, holding a scythe, reminiscent of the medieval representations of Death. But he too is always accompanied by the baby New Year.

Saturn's greatest festival was Saturnalia, held in December. Originally a rural festival held at the time of winter sowing, it spread. Very popular, it lasted seven days. All public and private business halted. Law courts and schools closed. Executions and military exercises were suspended. Slaves were temporarily freed and permitted to say and do as they pleased. The Romans went visiting, gave gifts of silver and gold objects, preserved fruits, cakes, candles and frankinsense, and clay or wax dolls, which were both vestiges of human sacrifice and offerings for good fortune. They decorated their homes with green boughs and trimmed trees with trinkets, toys and candles. They gambled and they feasted, gorging themselves on food and drink. The streets were filled with masked revellers riotously celebrating. This seasonal toleration of carousing is found also at New Year's Eve and Twelfth Night. Excessive indulgence continues today during the Mardi Gras in New Orleans and the Carnival in Rio de Janeiro.

In northern Europe, the ancient Scandinavians held the fire festival "Jul" to honor the god Thor, god of thunder, and the god Odin. The "jul log" or Yule log as we know it, a large and special log cut from a fruit bearing tree or a sacred oak, was ceremoniously burned at this time in many countries. This Yule log was the winter counterpart of the midsummer bonfires, kindled indoors instead of out in the cold. The Yule log represented the old sun. The lighting of it symbolized the rekindling of the weakened sun. Candles and torches were lit, indoors and out, to bring light to the darkness, turning night into day. As the yule log passed by, being hauled from the woods, it was good luck to doff one's hat. It was the custom to light the yule log fire with a fragment kept all year from the preceding year's log. The flames would hopefully burn out old wrongs and animosities.

THE YULE LOG

This tradition is still kept in a few areas. In Canada it is celebrated at the Empress Hotel in Victoria, B.C. On the evening of Christmas

Eve, the entrance of the Yule log is announced with great ceremony. The log is sprinkled with wine. The chef annoints it with fat (turkey drippings), and serving men place crossed hairs of a boar's head on the log as an emblem of good luck. Following tradition, the log is lit with a splinter of last year's log. There is singing, a fanfare and feasting.

In many places the lighting of the log was accompanied by prayers to ensure fertility in both women and animals. They would have, it was hoped, as many children, or chickens, lambs, and calves as there were sparks flying from shaken fragments of the log.

The fragments and ashes of the yule log also had the magical powers that those from the fires of the spring equinox. Pieces of the log were steeped in the water for the cows which then was supposed to cure them of any sickness, and help them calve. Ashes helped people. They were used to treat swollen glands and to prevent chilblains. Cold fragments were put under the bed to drive away rats and guard the house against danger. Ashes were sprinkled over the fields to promote the growth of crops. The part of the trunk which had been burnt in the fire was used to make the wedge for a new plough, which in turn would help the ground to be productive and the seeds to thrive. Even recently in parts of eastern Europe, the man of the house approached the fireplace and struck the blazing log. With each blow he wished for good health to the stock, to the land, and for a bountiful harvest.

Yule is connected with Guili, the Anglo Saxon name for December, and also a possible link with the Anglo-Saxon word hweol, meaning wheel. The wheel of the sun has completed its yearly cycle just as the wheel of the year has completed its revolution in time.

Other rituals were part of Solstice festivities. Making noise with bells and voices both greeted the light and the new year as well as frightening away evil spirits. We still "ring in the new year" with cheers, bells, and blowing of horns.

In northern Europe Odin, the king of the gods, was honoured with banquets and ceremonial drinking from enormous bowls.

Eskimos once held a big midwinter festival with dancing and gift-giving.

Jews celebrate Channukah, a midwinter Festival of Lights, when candles are lit on successive days until all the candles in the nine branched candelabra or menorah, are lit.

Christians celebrate Christmas, the birth of Jesus Christ, known as a light. He is also associated with death and resurrection or new life.

Even today we imitate the sun's light. Indoors and outdoors are decorated with lights, towns and cities from St. John's to Vancouver have tree lighting ceremonies, and ships in harbours are decorated with lights.

In England people once played a game called Snapdragon. Raisins were deposited in a large shallow bowl and brandy, or some other spirit, poured over the fruit and ignited. All lights in the room were extinguished, leaving only the eerie glow from the flaming brandy. Players, in turn, tried to grasp a raisin by plunging their hands through the flames. A variation on this game was to place a lighted candle in a can of ale and drink. Another custom, still in use, is the lighting of brandy poured over the special Christmas plum pudding.

Nineteenth century Newfoundlanders had their own version of Yule log traditions. As written in the ENCYCLOPEDIA OF NEWFOUNDLAND AND LABRADOR, in *"Newfoundland the log or "back junk" was cut before Christmas and, at sunset on Christmas Eve, placed at the back of the hearth. A blazing fragment was taken from the burning log at midnight on Christmas Eve and thrown over the house to protect it from danger of fire throughout the coming year."*

In 1785 George Cartwright described Christmas on the Labrador coast. *"At sunset the people ushered in Christmas according to the Newfoundland custom. In the first place they built a prodigious fire in their house, all hands assembled before the door, and one of them fired a gun loaded with powder only; afterwards each drank a dram of rum, concluding the ceremony with three cheers. These formalities being performed with great solemnity, they returned into their house, got drunk as fast as they could and spent the whole night in drinking, quarreling and fighting."* A few over exuberant Newfoundlanders were known to "shoot" the Christmas pudding out of the pot with a musket.

The holiday season is a time of cleaning house and baking, getting ready for the festivities and visitors. Mincemeat pies were originally rectangular in shape, and said to represent Christ's manger. The Puritans thought they were Popish and superstitious and ordered that the pies be altered. Many people believe we should eat mince pies by as many different cooks as possible; for every cook's pie, we will have a lucky month in the coming year.

Other cooking at this time, as today, included making fruitcakes and plum puddings, all of which were liberally laced with dried fruits and nuts, this then being the one time of year such luxuries could be afforded.

Oranges and nuts were also welcomed as gifts or as stocking presents.

It has been said that the farm animals have the gift of speech and they can talk on Christmas Eve. Some say that oxen kneel to pray. Bees are said to hum the one hundreth Psalm. Stock are given extra feed on this night and extra feed has been left out for the camels of the Wise Men or for Santa's reindeer. And milk and cookies are left out for Santa.

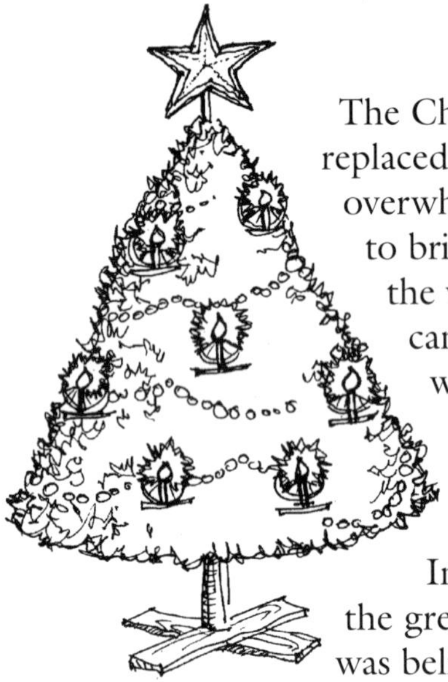

The Christmas tree custom came from Germany. An early Christian saint in Germany was said to have replaced an oak tree, sacred to the Celts, with a fir tree. Another story is that Martin Luther, being overwhelmed by the beauty of a night sky, cut a fir tree, brought it inside and trimmed it with candles to bring the lights of the stars inside. The evergreen trees and branches, remaining green throughout the winter, were symbols of long life and immortality. The custom of bringing the fir tree inside came to England from Germany with Prince Albert when he married Queen Victoria. Houses were not the only buildings decorated this way, churches too were festooned with greenery. This "Hanging of the Greens" is still a popular annual custom at many churches including the United Baptist Church in Sydney, Nova Scotia, which is packed by people of all faiths for this ceremony at Christmas time.

In the past mistletoe, a sacred plant of the ancient Greeks, Romans and Celts, was not included in the greenery because it was considered pagan. Mistletoe, ceremoniously cut once a year at this time, was believed to ward off evil spirits, cure illnesses, produce fertility and pacify one's enemies. Some of the pagan uses of mistletoe continue, such as kissing beneath it.

Today in North America, turkey is the most popular main course, followed by ham. In England until the Reformation the favorite was the traditional roast boar with the herb rosemary in its ears to represent the returning summer, and an apple in its mouth to represent the sun at this darkest time of the year. The boar's head was carried into the dining hall with great pomp and ceremony. The custom diminished but even today a boar's head, "bedecked with garlands of bay and rosemary" with an apple in its mouth is still ceremoniously served at Queen's College, Oxford University.

The Boar is dead
So, here is his head;
What man could have done more
Than his head off to strike,
Meleager like
And bring it as I do before?

The boar's head in hand bear I,
Bedecked with bays and rosemary;
And I pray you, my masters, be merry,
Quoit estis in convivio, (All you who are at this feast)
Caput apri defero, (I bear the boar's head,)
Redens laudes Domino. (giving thanks to the Lord)...

"The Boar's Head Carol"

Meleager, a hero of Greek legend, was distinguished for throwing the javelin and for slaying the Calydonian boar, a legendary ferocious beast that scourged the countryside.

The boar was sacred to Mars, as god of agriculture, and to Ceres (the Roman Demeter) and to Thor, Odin/Wodan and Freya, also a goddess of fertility. She accompanied Odin to the battlefield for she had the right to bring back to her palace one half of the warriors who died. Another Norse god, Freyr, god of peace and plenty, used to ride on a boar. His festival was held at the winter solstice, when a boar was sacrified to his honour.

The boar symbolized fertility and the harvest. In Greece a boar was sacrificed at the early Olympic Games and the athletes swore on pieces of the animal that they would compete fairly.

To Celts the boar was sacred, supernatural and magical, symbolizing the warrior and the hunt, as well as hospitality and fertility. The boar's head, containing the power of the life force and vitality, symbolized health and preservation from danger. Today, many pubs and inns in Britain are called "The Boar's Head".

Both Northern peoples and ancient Romans sacrificed swine. Bedecked with garlands of flowers and leaves the boar was led off to be sacrificed.

Today we have imitation pigs, piggy banks, which we "fatten" up with coins and then "slaughter" to retrieve them. The nursery rhyme "this little piggy went to market; this little piggy stayed home..." is also a selection process for sacrifice.

Once a sacrifical animal, the pig today occupies a different status. Gluttonous eaters are pigs; foul-mouthed men are pigs; to some, men in general are pigs. Pigs, on the other hand, seem to be more than just a barnyard animal. Even those three little pigs didn't stay home down on the farm. They went out into the world to build their own houses. One famous pig, Miss Piggy, is a TV and movie star; while another pig, Babe, is a talking pig who believes she is a sheep dog. The old boar, Major, in the book ANIMAL FARM, inspired the other pigs to revolt against their master and take over the farm. This took place on the Summer Solstice Eve, another key day of the year.

Santa has his roots in many figures. Odin, the northern Germanic warrior god, (Wodan as he's known in other parts) was also a patron of seers, poets and sorcerers. His powers surpassed all others. He was the most knowledgable and a master of magic, science and poetry. On stormy nights people believed they could hear him riding through the sky. Odin was also the god of war. A patron of warriors, he had a magic spear(made by dwarfs) and on his eight-legged horse he rode with the Valkyries to gather up those who have fallen in battle and carry them to Valhalla, the dead warriors' hall of honour. A master of disguises, Odin often travelled the world dressed as a simple wanderer, carrying a staff. He often dragged along a helper, a small dark and furry figure. This slave is the pagan, horned god,

Pan, the god of the hunt and king of the forest. Pan, the "dark one", sometimes dressed as a woman and he could be either a man or female or both in one. Carrying a broom or a thick rod, a symbol of masculine fertility, he threatened women and children. Also known as the devil or the bogey man, he represented the bestial side of sex and the darker side of man.

St. Nicholas, a bishop who lived in Asia Minor in the fourth century, wore a loose, hooded, fur trimmed robe. He distributed gifts to the poor and treats for the children. According to one story he threw pieces of gold down the chimney of a poor man's home and the coins landed in a stocking, hung to dry by the fire. So other people started hanging stockings by the fireplace. Good children could expect candies and such while naughty children might get only a lump of coal or a birch-rod for a spanking.

St. Nicholas, or Sinter Claus as he was known to the Dutch, came with them to North America. Washington Irving writes about him in his KNICKERBOCKER HISTORY OF NEW YORK. This inspired the English author, Clement Moore, in 1823 to write his now classic poem, "A Visit from St. Nicholas", which has imortalized Santa with the lines beginning "Twas the night before Christmas".

Later, St. Nicholas was pictured by a Bavarian-born illustrator with Harper's Magazine, Thomas Nast, as a fur-clad, small troll-like figure, quite unlike the tall Dutch St.Nicholas. He was assisted by a small gnome, dressed in animal skins and carrying a short broom-like rod to threaten boys and girls.

Our modern version of jolly old Santa comes from an 1931 Coca Cola advertisement. He is dressed in red, trimmed with fur. He is fat and jolly and helped by cute little elves. This Santa drives a sleigh pulled by reindeer through the sky. In doing this he is similar to ancient sun gods who drove their chariots pulled by horses or rode in boats across the sky and were celebrated at the Winter Solstice.

The stories of St. Nicholas also arrived in North America with German settlers. Sometimes one figure, he was also known to be two distinct people: Krishkrinkle and Pelsnichol. One rewarded good children, the other punished the bad. If anyone was naughty he would find a birch-rod instead of candy. The name Pelsnichol, or "Nicholas with the fur", alluded to the dress of skins which he wore. A vestige of this is celebrated today in Lunenburg County, Nova Scotia. Although popular for many years, barely a handful of people of German descent now continue to "belsnickle", usually on the day after Christmas. Masked and disguised in costumes, they play music, sing, make merry and receive treats, usually a drink of rum, from the houses they are entertaining. Belsnickling is similar to old English mummering, in which people dress up and go from door to door singing and performing.

The Celts went "guising", dressed up in animal skins and often wearing horns or antlers on their heads, accompanied by boys dressed as old women. They ran around and were frequently hit with sticks by villagers. These were part of the old Hogmanay celebrations of the Cetic sun god Hogmagog. The origin of the name is obscure. One derivation is from the ancient Scandinavian for the night preceding the feast of Yule and refers to the animals slaughtered for sacrificial or feasting purposes. In Scotland and northern England, a hogg is the name of a yearling lamb, while in other parts, a hogg is a year old pig, including a wild boar. Both the lamb and the boar were sacrificial animals.

Another possible derivation of the word Hogmanay is from "Au gui menez" - "to the mistletoe go", alluding to the ceremony of gathering that sacred plant. Hogmanay also refers to the special oat cake given to the children, who go around much as modern children do at Halloween.

Today, Hogmanay, celebrated on New Year's Eve, is a time of wishing others good luck and a hope for a happy and hopeful New Year. It is a time for families and neighbours. In Edinburgh, celebrations are more elaborate and are believed to be the biggest New Year Party in the world. This Hogmanay Festival continues to grow in strength and popularity. Over four days, revellers enjoy an opening torchlight parade and fire festival, several concerts, street theatres, many other events and an epic street party on Hogmanay night itself. Young people, and those young in heart, have been gathering annually for the past few years. At Hogmanay 1996/97, four hundred thousand or so came together to celebrate the beginning of a New Year.

Once there were groups of "guisers", singing, dancing, feasting and drinking at the homes they visited. And a "rude and grotesque drama" was performed. Bonfires were lit and burning wheels of straw rolled down hills, imitating the movement of the sun as did celebrations at the Summer Solstice. Blazing torches were tossed. One ancient custom was to ignite animal hides wrapped around sticks; the resulting smoke was said to ward off evil spirits.

In one Scottish village, Burhead, on the southern shore of the Moray Firth, an ancient ceremony, the burning of the Clavie, was still being performed in the 1860s. A large tar barrel was sawn into uneven parts. The smaller end being used as the foundation of the Clavie and the larger end being broken up for fuel. A four foot fir prop, the spoke, was secured into a bored hole and staves from a herring cask were set out around the clavie base at two inch intervals, leaving a large aperature for a man's head. The other ends were attached to the pole. Wood and tar and other combustible materials were poured and packed into the barrel until they rose about a foot over the rim and were then set on fire.

A man, Clavie bearer one, put his head between the staves and ran, carrying the Clavie through the village. He was followed by the shouting villagers and "with the boiling tar meanwhile trickling down in dark sluggish streams over his back." If he stumbled it could mean death for him and augered disaster for the village in the coming year. As another bearer took his place, the crowd grabbed for flaming firebrands. A succession of bearers ran the Clavie to the top of a hill, where it was set on a special "altar" and more fuel added to the fire. Then the barrel was hurled down the western slope, so the hill looked like a mass of flames. Villagers raced for the embers and brands, which were kept for good luck. (R.Chambers...THE BOOK OF DAYS.1866)

Bizarre fire festivities are still held today in Paraguay on St. John the Baptist Day, June 24, the middle of their winter when the days are shortest and the sun the weakest. Candles are lit on sidewalks and in trees. Dummies filled with fireworks are set on scaffolds and set on fire. Balls of fire, unravelling strands of flames, are kicked around the streets. Men with frameworks of bulls with flaming heads and tails held over their heads and shoulders rush about frightening the crowds of people. Games of fortune telling are played. Will I marry? Who will I marry? But the ultimate test of faith is to walk barefoot over glowing hot coals.

In Sweden, on December 13, the date of the Winter Solstice under the old Julian calendar, Lucia's Day, girls dress in white and wear wreaths of lighted candles on their heads. In homes, the eldest daughter plays the part of Lucia, wakes everyone in the household, bringing coffee and saffron buns in shapes of goats' horns and wagon wheels. Her sisters follow, carrying lighted candles, while the brothers wear white cone-shaped caps decorated with stars. According to legend, Lucia, a young third century Christian saint, came from her native Sicily to Sweden in the midst of a great famine to bring food. Arriving in the dark of night she was dressed in white and stood at the helm of a brilliantly lighted ship laden with food. This embodies a more ancient and pagan ritual performed at the Winter Solstice for the return of sunlight. Even Lucia's name means "light". Today, combining a religious and secular event, many schools and communities have Lucia processions and the custom is becoming more popular.

Similar to the old Hogmanay celebrations was "Oidhche Na Calluinn", performed as late as the 1950's on Cape Breton's North Shore. Groups of people used it as a way of collecting food for the needy. Carrying lanterns, they travelled in sleighs and on snowshoes to various homes. Here, the leader of the group with a sheepskin over his head, ran around the house three times in the direction of the sun while another man ran behind beating the skin and making loud noises. A special verse was recited. The food collected was taken to a home where it was needed, perhaps one where the father had died that year. A feast was served to the group and there was a dance. The house was filled with merrymaking and plenty of food was left for the family.

The customs of masquerading or mummering are ancient. At the Roman Saturnalia, men and women dressed in the clothing of the opposite sex, and wore masks of all kinds. The early Christians on the Feast of the Circumcision, or New Year's Day, ran around in masks in ridicule of pagan superstitions.

In medieval England and later, and in other parts of Europe bands of men and women, especially at Christmas time, dressed in fantastic clothes and wore masks and serenaded people outside their houses or joined the revelry inside. Many were disguised as bears and unicorns or wore deerhides and antlers or ram's horns.

Henry VII, alarmed at the excesses of these celebrations, issued an ordinance against mummering and declared that all persons who went about houses arrayed in this fashion were liable to be arrested as vagabonds, committed to jail for three months, and fined at the king's pleasure. The reason was the number of murders and other crimes committed while the merrymakers were disguised.

To shorten winter's sadness,
See where the folks with gladness
Disguised all are coming,
Right wantonly a-mumming.
Fa la.
"La Musa Madrigalesca"

English mummering, or mumming, was brought to Newfoundland by Sir Humphrey Gilbert in 1583. In 1842 J.B. Jukes described: *"Men, dressed in all kinds of fantastic disguises, and some in women's clothes, with gaudy colours and painted faces, and generally armed with a bladder full of pebbles tied to a kind of whip, paraded the streets, playing practical jokes on each other and on the passers by, performing rude dances, and soliciting money or grog. They called themselves Fools and Mummers..."*

R.H.Bonnycastle in 1842 *"noted the existence of a play which "they perform, at those houses which admit them...It is a dialogue between the captain and a sailor...and a mock fight goes on...till one is supposed to be slain, when the doctor is called in to bring him to life again."*, resembling the Punch and Judy puppet shows.

"Gerald M.Sider (1974) established the existence of two forms of mummering in nineteenth century Newfoundland, which emerged as a result of social dichotomy and the rapidly increasing distinction between urban and rural environments. Urban practices, particularly at St. John's, tended to be strictly organized, involving large groups in parades. Mummering, however, was often abused: the use of disguises permitted those of poorer classes to harass the wealthy merchant classes or often allowed rival religious sects the opportunity to vent their hostility while in masquerade."

In 1860 a man in Conception Bay was murdered by someone in disguise and this prompted the authorities to prohibit *"the wearing of any disguise or mask in a public place in Newfoundland without direct permission of a magistrate ...(the law) was subsequently responsible for the extinction of mummering at St. John's on pain of a sentence of seven days or twenty shillings."*

But mummering has returned. It continues in Newfoundland and mummering workshops were given in the 1970s in the St. John's area. Today, small informal groups of disguised revellers entertain friends and neighbours at Christmastime.

Mummers in England performed the story of St. George and the Dragon. St. George tells of his exploits with the dragon and he challenges any man to stand up to him. The first is a Turkish knight, enemy of the Christian crusader, who is cut down "like the evening sun". The Doctor appears and restores him. "Rise dead man." Then there is another challenger, and again he is cut down and restored to life. Challengers also included Oliver

Cromwell, whose followers killed the king, and Beelzebub, second only to Satan. This traditional play, mimics the life cycle of nature with its life, death and rebirth.

In another Christmas theatrical production, the English Pantomime performed today, there are two levels of entertainment - one for the children, the other laced with sexual overtones for the adults. The biggest laughs are for men disguised as women and the cheers are for the hero, always a woman disguised as a man.

Another pastime of the holiday season has been to play the game, Blindman's Buff, in which one person is blindfolded and he must reach out and choose another person to be "it". Here we have another vestige of choosing "victims".

What are all these remnants of solstice celebrations? Are they memories of actual events we have tucked away in the back of our collective unconsciousness? What if on the day after the Winter Solstice the sun did not come back? There are myths and stories around the world that tell of awesome events, of when angry sky gods hurled fire down to earth, when the sun disappeared, and when a great flood destroyed most of mankind.

There is a Japanese legend in which people witnessed an unusually brilliant sunset one evening. And when they awoke, there was no sun. It was said that the sun had argued with her brother, a sea god, and she was hiding in a cave. Time passed. The climate got colder; lakes and rivers froze; crops failed; people died. Finally the sun was tricked into returning. Litle by little she edged out of her cave.

The Roman poet, Ovid, writes of the Greek legend of the boy Phaeton, who sought out his father, the sun god. Helios/Apollo offered to grant any wish the boy made. Phaeton asked to drive the chariot of the sun across the sky. The father tried to dissuade him, but the boy insisted.

When he got into the chariot the horses knew he was a different and a weaker driver. The boy struggled to keep them on course as they hurtled crazily, wheeling and plunging, through the sky. *"As ships on the sea will skitter without their usual ballast, yawing and rolling, the Sun's chariot bounces along, unstable, a bobbling plaything...*

"The earth bursts into flame, the crests of the mountains first, and then, as the moisture of rocks comes to a sudden boil, in loud, random explosions. Trees are consumed, and grain in an instant ripens to ash.

"Try to imagine," writes Ovid, *"entire cities consumed in a moment, the nightmare of whole nations flashing, charring, gone. The woodland is burning, and mountains are smouldering logs in a huge hearth that is the world...the smoke and sparks are a dreadful whirl on all sides as heaven turns into hell...*

"Phaeton's eyeballs fry, and his lids are all but seared together, but, could he open his eyes, it would do no good in the choking soot and smoke. It was then that the Ethiopians, up until then like us, were blackened by the intense heat, and Libya turned from a garden spot to the desert we see there now as her rivers and lakes were boiled away...

"And the world's great rivers shrank in their beds and died... Water birds...poach... The seven mouths of the Nile choke with dust and die...

"The ocean itself, enraged, skulked off to leave behind it an enormous desolation of cooked fish in the baking mud. There were brand-new islands, hiterto submerged but now towering high in the nightmare landscape, mountains where the only game was the upturned bellies of dead dolphins." The air was on fire; the oceans boiled.

The Earth was in agony. Twice she shuddered and then sank lower. She pleaded with the king of the gods to help. "Fighting fire with fire" he hurled a lightning bolt across the sky and hit Phaeton. The boy, his hair ablaze, fell to Earth in a fiery ball, trailing *"fire and smoke behind him"*.

His father mourned over the boy's death and it was a long time before he once again drove his chariot across the sky. *"If we believe the stories we have heard passed down from these times, there was once an entire day when the Sun never appeared, and the only light was the garish glare from those still burning fields and woods."*

Phaeton means "blazing star" and it was a general belief that he was placed in the heavens by Zeus/Jupiter and became the planet Venus, the morning and evening star.

From all around the world there are stories and astronomical records of a blazing star appearing suddenly in the sky, and which disturbed the movement of the sun, and led to conflagration of the earth. Venus is described as having sprung from the head of Jupiter. and being erratic and unstable in the sky before finding her place. She is described as having a glowing train, of being a smoking star, a serpent cloud, a pillar of smoke, a dragon. The Babylonian goddess Astarte was known as "the bright torch of heaven". Ishtar appeared and the heavens "trembled" and the "earth quaked". Athena appeared suddenly in the sky, sprung from the head of Zeus/Jupiter and the sky "reeled", earth "trembled" and "shrieked". The goddesses associated with Venus, sometimes represented as dragons, or with serpents, are pictured with horns. The word comet comes from the Latin and Greek meaning wearing long hair, a long haired star.

In ancient Mexico the sun was attacked by Quetzal-cohuatl. After the disappearance of this feathered serpent-shaped body, the sun refused to shine for four days. Thereafter the snakelike body transformed itself into a great star, appearing for the first time in the east. Many people died of famine and pestilence.

After the appearance of Venus, the days were longer, the sun in a different position.

Over the Pacific in Hawaii, a hero Maui had set a trap for the sun and caught it in a noose. It could not escape. The hero attacked the sun with a magic weapon. The sun begged for mercy and agreed to go more slowly through the sky. The days grew longer.

The sun was captured and attacked by other heroes. One noose caught it around the neck and choked the sun until the sky darkened, then the noose was cut and the sun could breathe again. The sun has also been swallowed as well as being snared by a net and eaten.

In the sequence of the myths there followed great battles in the sky involving the sun, the moon and the planets Venus and Mars. The sky was filled with fire-breathing dragons, witches flying on broomsticks, and great monsters and gods and goddesses fighting each other. The planet Mars looked like a warrior holding a sword.

The book of Exodus in the Bible recounts the efforts of Moses and the Jews to escape from Egypt. The Lord gave Moses a magic rod, that turned into a serpent. Each time Moses or his brother Aaron stretched out his hand and lifted the rod another plague in a series of plagues began. The first time the rod struck the waters of the Nile, *"and all the water...turned to blood. And the fish died; and the Nile became foul, so that the Egyptians could not drink water from the Nile."*

"Frogs came up and covered the land. The frogs died out of the houses and courtyards and out of the fields. And they gathered them together in heaps, and the land stank." The rod *"struck the dust of the earth, and there came gnats on man*

and beast...and then came great swarms of flies...and a very severe plague upon ... cattle which are in the field, the horses, the asses, the camels, the herds, and the flocks."

Ashes thrown towards heaven *"became boils breaking out in sores on man and beast...and thunder and hail, and fire ran down to the earth...there was hail, and fire flashing continually in the midst of the hail....The hail struck down everything that was in the field throughout all the land."*

"And the locusts came up over all the land of Egypt, and...they covered the face of the whole land, so that the land was darkened, and they ate all the plants in the land and all the fruits of the trees which the hail had left; not a green thing remained..."

Then Moses stretched out his hand toward heaven and, *"there was thick darkness in all the land of Egypt three days."*

The plagues didn't stop there. The Lord was to destroy the first born of man and beast but the Jews would be saved if they sacrificed a male lamb a year old (from a sheep or a goat). They were to sacrifice all on the same evening and smear the blood on the lintels of their houses. They were to eat the roasted lamb, with unleavened bread and bitter herbs. Then the Lord "passed over" the homes of the Jews as he destroyed the first born of the Egyptians.

The next day the Jews started to leave *"and the Lord went before them by day in a pillar of cloud to lead them along the way, and by night in a pillar of fire to give them light."*

But the Egyptians pursued them. The pillar of cloud, the "angel of God", moved between the Jews and the Egyptians. The rod was used again. This time *"the Lord drove the sea back by a strong east wind all night, and made the sea dry land, and the waters were divided."*

Pharoah and his men followed but were destroyed as the waters came back upon them.

There followed years of darkness, filled with desolation, warfare and plagues. One day *"the sun stayed in the midst of heaven, and did not hasten to go down for about a whole day"*. Joshua held out his javelin and the cities of enemies were destroyed.

Other celestial events announced what appeared to be the end of the world. Many people adopted the philosophy *"Let us eat and drink, for tomorrow we die." "The Lord of hosts is mustering a host for battle. They come from a distant land, from the end of the heavens...to destroy the whole Earth....For the stars of the heavens and their constellations will not give their light; the sun will be dark at its rising and the moon will not shed its light."*

"The inhabitants of the earth are scorched, and few men are left...For the windows of heaven are opened, and the foundations of the earth tremble. The earth is utterly broken, the earth is rent assunder, the earth is violently shaken."

A Germanic myth believed that, after a terrible battle the sun will set fire to the world. The sun will turn black, the earth sink into the sea, and the bright stars fall from the sky.

Biblical Judgement Day *"will come like a thief; on it the heavens will pass away with a roar, the heavenly bodies will burn up and be destroyed, and the earth and all its works will melt away."*

Other people around the world have foreseen similar ends to the world, a series of catastophes which include floods, earthquakes, fire and darkness.

These accounts have been passed down through the ages and today are no more than stories. However, many of the descriptions may be a mythic way of describing actual physical events.

Astronomers around the world watched the heavens meticulously, and had to readjust calendars and celestial charts. Temples and monuments, whose foundations were aligned to the sun, were overlaid with properly realigned new foundations.

We know there have been a series of Ice Ages. The ice itself was a major catastrophe, but as the ice retreated the earth heaved violently as the weight of ice was released. As a result the sea level rose abruptly and massive flooding occurred. There are many accounts of a major universal flood around the world. Accompanying these were violent earthquakes and volcanic activity, giant windstorms and rains of fire.

There were violent swings in climate. More than once the earth was said to have tumbled, reversing its magnetic poles. There was lightning and "the burning of heaven", which caused the earth to be turned upside down or "heaven and earth to change places". "The earth swaggered like a drunken man, it sways like a hut." Many people believed that a natural catastrophe, in particular a comet, would cause the earth to "turn over".

Land became sea and sea became land. Lush land turned into deserts or were buried under ice and snow.

There were massive extinctions of animals and the destruction of civilizations. One explanation for the extinction of the dinosaurs some sixty five million years ago, long before man was on earth, is that a giant asteroid or meteor hit the

Earth, causing earthquakes, volcanic activity, which in turn caused climatic change, burning heat and raining fire as the Earth caught on fire. The sun was blocked by volcanic dust particles and the earth was plunged into darkness. Lakes and rivers froze. Plants stopped growing. Food supply diminished.

There is evidence of several sudden catastrophes. Mammoths in Siberia died so suddenly that they were frozen still chewing on grass. Broken and splintered bones of tropical animals have been found in northern Europe. Hippopotamus, reindeer, elephants, tigers in England and Wales, while crocodiles and fresh water tortoises are found below limestone containing marine, salt-water shells in Paris.

Whales were in Michigan, while a mixture of extinct and other animals in fissures in rocks were found in Wales and western Europe, the bones still in a fresh state. Saber-tooth tigers, camels, horses, mammoths and peacocks are smashed and mangled with each other in the La Brea tar pits in Los Angeles. Human bones and artifacts (pottery,tools) have been discovered mixed with bones of extinct animals in Florida. These later fossil beds were deposited between two and four thousand years ago.

Petrified forests are found in the desolate polar sea off the coast of Siberia. The remains of exotic plants, fig trees and magnolias are in Greenland; water lilies and other luxuriant tropical plants and coral are discovered now in coal deposits in Antartica and in Spitzbergen in the Arctic Ocean. The fossils of tropical ferns are in the coal of Cape Breton. Are these simply consequences of continental drift or are there further explanations?

Recently, an American scholar, John Anthony West, concluded that the erosion of the Sphinx and other desert monuments in Egypt was caused by water rather than by wind. And, although many do not agree with him, this amount of the water could only have occured during the great rains and flooding at the end of the last Ice Age between 13,000 BC and 10,500 BC (eleventh millennium BC) after which in continuing climatic shifts and cataclysms, the green savannah turned into the dry Sahara.

Others, like the Beligian engineer Robert Blauval, using archeo-astronomical methods and studying the astronomical alignments of ancient monuments and buildings have also pushed back the time-frame of civilizations. By suggesting earlier dates for high civilizations, questions arise as well as a new and challenging look at history.

The abandonned "ghost" city of Tiahuanaco in the mountains of Bolivia was a thriving port as far back, Graham Hancock and others believe, as 15,000 BC. Elephants and bizarre animals are carved into walls there. Although numerous at one time, these animals became extinct in the Andes around 10,000 BC. Disaster struck. The climate became colder, sea levels rose, and the people abandonned the city.

Minoan civiliation in Crete was destroyed in successive waves between 1800 and 1500 BC, one of them being the same time as a series of plagues caused destruction, and the Red Sea "parted", allowing the Jews to escape from Egypt, as described in the book of Exodus in the Bible.

In 1883 on the Indonesian island of Krakatau a volcano erupted causing two thirds of the island to disappear while the resulting sea waves caused the deaths of about thirty six thousand people. Clouds of volcanic dust distorted the atmosphere and also caused brilliant sunsets around the world. The skies were noticeably darker for over two years. If Krakatau caused the skies to darken, the effects of several Krakataus at different places would cause the sun to "disappear'. Effects would be devastating locally and worldwide.

The eruption of Mount Pinatubo in the Phillipines in 1991 lowered the climate of the planet by about one half a degree, killed over three hundred people and caused mudsliding and displacement of one hundred thousand people. A more recent eruption in Iceland lowered the climate by almost a degree.

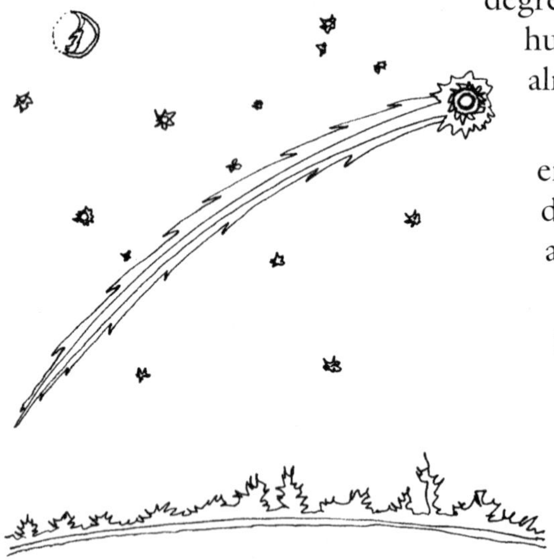

Recent natural disasters, floods, hurricanes, tornadoes, earthquakes and volcanic eruptions, have involved people living not only in rural far off countries, but next door in trailer parks, subdivisons and cities. Their effects have caused such comments as "Apocolyptic" and "destructive to the human psyche".

Sky "shows" of meteorite showers and comets have long been believed to be forerunners of disaster.

"If it once be admitted that comets distemper and inflame the air, and exhaust the succus (juices) of the Earth, it will necessarily follow, that a barren soil, and the corrupting and blasting of the fruits must be the products of them: and from these will naturally ensue death, scarcity and famine. And, as the inevitable effect of both, we must expect sickness, diseases, mortality, and more especially the sudden death of many Great Ones, because these are sooner and more easily hurt than others, for their delicate feeding, and luxurious course of life, and sometimes their great cares and watchings, which weaken and infeeble their bodies, render them more obnoxious than the vulgar sort of people." (COMETOMANTIA 1684)

The word "disaster" itself is associated with the sky and means an unfavorable aspect of a star or "obnoxious" planet; an evil star. Obnoxious orginally meant exposed to harm and injury, subject to injury or evil of any kind. The tail of the comet was believed to be poisonous.

Comets have been studied for centuries by astrologers and astronomers around the world. The study included fortune telling, which was usually for important people, and generally meant bad news. Comets also brought with them bad news for the general public.

Plagues, wars and upheavals of society were the result. People themselves added to the belief that comets were dangerous. Many killed themselves to save the comet the trouble. In the year 999 a general hysteria possessed people in Europe. Believing that the end of the world was imminent pilgrims flocked to Jerusalem to await Judgement Day. Many sold their properties. Buildings were allowed to fall into ruin or were purposefully destroyed. Why repair when the end of the world was at hand? Each storm produced terror. Thunder was believed to be the voice of God.

The belief that comets augered disaster was reinforced in England by the appearance of a comet just before the Norman Invasion of 1066.

Many attributed the Great Black Death Plague to the appearance of comets.

The Incas of Peru believed the damage from comets to be the anger of their sun god. When celestial events foretold imminent disaster, human beings were sacrificed to placate the gods and hopefully to stop the impending catastrophes.

A few years ago people eagerly awaited the arrival of the comet Kaoutek, but were disappointed when it made a poor showing in the sky. Perhaps we should thank our lucky stars that it fizzled out.

1997 saw the appearance of another comet, Hale-Bopp. This one was clearly observed. The year also had a series of disasters. People living in North Dakota and Manitoba were devastated by the worst spring floods in years; residents of Montserrat in the West Indies watched the approaching fireflows from a volcano that had never erupted in recorded history and which destroyed property and dislocated the population of the entire island; and Maritime farmers had to plow under several acres of vegetable crops because of the driest July on record.

Now scientists are warning of the largest climatic event of the century as el Nino arrives. The waters of the Pacific are warming and this leads to weather changes around the world. This happens roughly every seven years, but never like this. It is threatening to be the strongest and largest el Nino in the last one hundred fifty years.

It will cause tidal waves in Chili and Peru, flooding in the southern United States, and on the other side of the

Pacific, drought in Southeast Asia and destructive brushfires there and in Australia. An el Nino in 1982/83 caused over eight billion dollars damage and two thousand deaths. This one is expected to rival or surpass it.

Superstitious people in earlier generations would have argued that the appearance of the comet, Hale-Bopp, gave advance warning of these natural disasters.

In the event that the legends are accounts of actual physical disasters, little wonder that people have gone to extremes at certain key times of the year to placate the gods, to offer human sacrifice, to imitate the sun, and to disguise themselves from Death.

Perhaps people subconsciously remember ancient disasters but are far enough removed from them that instead of hurling burning wheels of straw down hills they decorate with Christmas lights; and our nursery rhymes and Valentines are for pleasure and not for choosing a sacrificial victim who will ensure our survival by placating the gods.

Boxing Day is an English custom. Originally boxes were kept in the churches for donations for special masses to be said. The box at Christmas-time was the Christmas box and this held more donations. They were opened the day after Christmas. Over the years, the money was spent, not only for masses, but given to the poor themselves. Later, tradesmen, servants and children went "boxing", soliciting tips from householders they had served during the year. Today many still give extra donations to the needy at this time and bonuses for the milkman and others who assisted us throughout the year.

At the holiday season the punch bowl comes out of the cupboard. Egg nog is one of the favorites and the word "nog" is an abbreviation of noggin, a small wooden pitcher made from one block of wood in which holiday drinks were once served.

Silibub was another holiday drink of which originally only the foam was served. Its mildness made it a lady's drink, while the gentlemen gathered in an adjoining room around the more alcoholic punch bowl.

Christmas drinks of the past were much richer in protein than they were in alcohol. Wassail is one of the traditional drinks. Wassail is the Anglo-Saxon word meaning "Be whole, be well" and is equivalent to "Here's your health". The Wassail bowl was a special bowl, often of massive silver and frequently decorated with ribbons and rosemary. The large bowl was carried from house to house by carollers, who expected the householders to fill it.

Wassail is also the song or carol sung by the wassailers as well as the person singing and drinking and the drink itself. People can still "keep wassail", and carouse and drink, even though it's not with the old-fashioned wassail.

Long ago people wassailed not only family and friends but also their cattle and their fruit trees. People drank to their health so they would thrive and produce more.

Wassaile the trees
That they may bear
You many a plum
And many a pear.

One way to wassail the apples trees was to go out carrying torches, with family and friends and a large pitcher of wassail or hot cider, encircle the biggest and most productive tree, as representaive of the rest, and drink a special toast three times. Then sprinkle the tree with cider, or dash a bowl of cider against it. "O tree. O tree. O tree. Bear fruit and flourish. Thy owner nourish. Give wealth and plenty." Then the party would move on to the next farm.

A more ancient custom was for someone, at midnight on Christmas Eve, to go naked into the orchard and bind the trees with ropes of straw, thus asking for productivity from both the fruit trees and the grain harvest.

Punch is a comparatively modern drink and it came to us from India in the late 1600s. Punch comes from the Hindustani word paunch, meaning five, the number of ingredients usually required to form the mixture. However, some use only four ingredients:

When'er a bowl of punch we make
Four striking opposites we take -
The strong, the weak, the sour, the sweet,
Together mixed most kindly meet.

During the 1600s sailors drank "paunch" but during the next century rum was added and the name became, more appropriately, "punch".

We do not use a toasted biscuit anymore, but it used was once a favorite addition to the many old English drinks.

It was from this use of toasted bread or biscuit that we get the word toast, as applied in the first instance, to a beautiful woman whose health is often drunk; and then to the act of drinking the health of any person or to any idea or sentiment.

At the holiday time it is, as an ancient Roman philosopher said, "not so much the pleasure of eating and drinking as that of finding oneself among his friends and conversing with them". Times have not changed much.

Should auld acquaintance be forgot,
And never brought to min'?
Should auld acquaintance be forgot,
And auld lang syne?

For auld lang syne, my dear,
For auld lang syne,
We'll tak a cup of kindness yet,
For auld lang syne.
by Robert Burns

JANUARY

This month is named after the double-faced Roman god Janus, who looked back towards the old year and forward to the new year. He presided over doors and gateways and over the first hour of the day, the first day of the month and this first month of the year. He is the god of beginnings.

Gaelic, "An ceud Mhios na Bliadhna" - "First Month of the Year"; Micmac "Punamu'juiku's" - "Tomcod appearing"; Saxon, "Wolf Month" because the cold drove the wolves from the forests to the villages looking for food; also known as the "Snow Month". The full moon is "Wolf Moon".

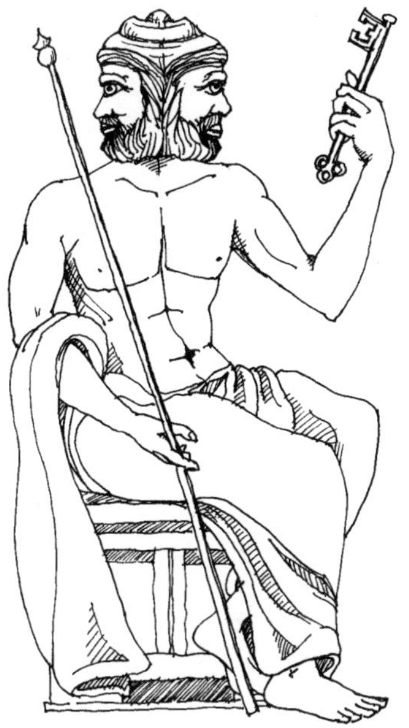

Sing a song of seasons;
Something bright in all...
by Robert Louis Stevenson.

Ring out the old, ring in the new,
Ring, happy bells, across the snow;
The year is going, let him go;
Ring out the false, ring in the true.
"In Memorium CVI" by Alfred Lord Tennyson

There are many traditions about greeting the New Year. It's a time of rejoicing, celebrating, and blowing horns and ringing bells. The devils of the old year were frightened away and kept from following into the new.

In England doors of houses were opened to let the old year out and the new year in. It was good luck if a chimney sweep cleaned the slates on the roofs of houses. Hence the saying that a person can start the new year with a "clean slate".

It is a time of visiting and exchanging gifts. First footing, or "first foot in" was practised by Scots and English. It was hoped that the first person to enter a house after midnight would be a black-haired man, bearing a gift of food, thus ensuring a year of prosperity and good luck.

January 6 is Old Christmas or Twelfth Night.

The main event commemorated is the visit of the Three Wise Men from the East who followed a star to the baby Jesus arriving twelve days after his birth. They brought gifts, gold representing royalty, frankincense symbolizing his divinity, and myrrh used in the embalming process and thus symbolizing imortality.

An ancient Babylonian festival which went on for twelve days at this time was a festival of the fates, a ritual which involved looking at the omens for each of the twelve months to come.

The Greek fates, also goddesses of spinning, made their rounds dispensing good or bad fortune during the twelve nights. But they allowed no spinning during that time. It was their task to spin the fortunes of mankind with the threads of destiny. They determined the destiny of every human being. This destiny was symbolized by a thread, which at a birth the first of the Fates drew from the distaff of her spinning wheel, the second wound, and the third cut the thread when the span of life that it represented was over.

St. Distaff's day is on January 12, but there is no St. Distaff. The day was named for the staff on which wool or flax was wound for spinning. On this day the women returned to their spinning after the holiday season. Spinning was considered a suitable pastime for ladies because it "stoppeth a gap and saveth a woman from being idle". A wife is known as the distaff side in a marriage. Unmarried women in a family often were given the chore of spinning, hence they were known as spinsters.

At Twelfth Night in Europe, as in ancient Rome, slaves, servants and students reversed their social positions. They were allowed to "lord it over" their masters. For one day someone could play a king, or a bishop, and become the Lord of Misrule. Men dressed up as devilish figures with frightening masks or wore animal skins.

The custom of electing a mock king of the feast for a day was derived from ancient Greece or the Near East. A gold coin or a bean or pea was baked in a special cake. Whoever found it was made Lord of Misrule, king of the feast, king of the day, king of the bean. He advised all present to make fools of themselves. He then chose his queen and their court. The chief entertainment was drinking which led to excesses and abuse of the celebration. Ancient Roman children at the end of Saturnalia drew lots with beans to see who would be king. These festivities took the place of a still more ancient custom of choosing a victim to be sacrificed.

Early January is a quiet time after the busy holidays, a time to recover from feasting and partying. This may have been the reason early Saxons believed that early January was an unlucky time. They were convinced that if anyone drank on Jan 2 he would die within fifteen days. It was also a bad time to get sick or hurt, to work or marry.

Ice skating has long been a popular winter sport. Years ago stock or block skates were made. Two blocks of ash wood were preferred. Attached to the blocks was a bar of quarter inch by one inch Swedish steel, although children's skates often used an old rasp for the blade, held on by wire and a few screws. Later came the spring skates which clipped onto the shoe, and still later by the shoe skates we know today.

It was said that a generation or so ago the ice on Sydney Harbour would be literally "black" with people enjoying themselves. Skating and ice-boating, car and horse racing, all brought people onto the ice.

Other winter sports are sledding, snowshoeing, and skiing - both downhill and cross-country. One questionable winter game played was to see who could lick the largest hole in the ice.

Winter made doing the laundry an extra challenge. If there was no running water, a lot of snow had to be melted. Clothes were usually dried on rods and racks by the wood range in the kitchen. If the clothes were hung outside they immediately froze and became hard to handle.

A few rooms were shut off from the rest of the house and not used again until the warmer weather.

Firewood was often cut in the winter. The hard-packed snow made hauling logs easier and the cut logs could then be left to dry out. When burned later in the year, or the next winter, they gave off a better heat and were less liable to cause creasote to accumulate in the chimney - something we are well aware of today.

Years ago cutting firewood was a community project. At Ingonish Centre, as in many communities, the logs were cut and hauled to a person's house. The wood would be chopped from 9 pm to about 2:30 am, then fiddle music was played and people danced until daylight. This ritual continued until everyone had the winter's supply of wood. In later years a portable sawmill was taken around the countryside to saw wood into stovelengths.

For the hottest and longest lasting heat, beech is considered the best, followed by maple. Birch looks nice in the woodpile and stacked by the fireplace but the heat is not as intense and the bark gives off an oily smoke. Even well dried alders give a good heat. Dried spruce or fir is good for summer fires because it catches fast and gives sufficient heat for cooking without overheating the kitchen for the rest of the day.

Handy hint - a handful of sugar sprinkled over the coals and the fire will light faster.

Today we still superstitiously knock on wood three times to ward off bad luck. This derives from the ancient belief that certain trees were sacred and could keep them from harm. When a person wanted to ask a favour of the god who lived there, he would touch the bark. If the favour was granted he would thank the god by knocking on the tree. The number three is a magic number.

Winter added hardships to travelling. Roads were often impassable. It was a difficult chore to "break a road", using the best horse out in front to make a narrow track, and snow brigades of men also shovelled tracks. Some summer roads were not used during the winter because the snow drifted too high; winter tracks were made instead across fields. Sometimes the snow was so high a person's head would touch the telegraph wires.

Roads were made across the lakes and harbour, and local governments were responsible for "bushing" the ice on major thoroughfares across the Bras d'Or Lakes and Sydney Harbour. To "bush the ice" spruce trees were stuck in holes in the ice at regular intervals between land points to serve as a guideline. Without these bushes as guides, it would have been impossible to cross the ice in stormy weather. Even with these precautions, during a severe storm visibility was limited and it was all too easy to lose sight of the bushes and become lost.

By the winter of 1949-50 the roads had been improved in the rural areas and snowploughs were used regularly.

When the roads were especially bad, either with snow or mud, and impassable very little farm produce got to market, causing supplies to run low and cost more.

Agricultural production was much greater in local areas early in the century. In 1929, for example, there was heavy shipping of food to Sydney from Inverness County. On one February day over one thousand pounds of dressed poultry were sent down. On another day Mabou shipped over two thousand pounds altogether of chicken, geese and turkeys. An Egg Circle in St. Joseph du Moine shipped ten boxes (over five hundred pounds) of chickens, and there were also shipments of chickens from the Margaree Valley.

Household journal of David Edward Nicholl, of Gabarus.

JANUARY - 1894

1. In the evening We all went to Mr Stacy and to tea.
2. Helping W. Hardy move a barn. Snow about 10 inches deep.
3. the same
4. Helping William Hardy put the roof on the barn. Shod the mare.
5. Killed three sheep. Wesley Nicoll went to Sydney. Fine day.
6. Killed a lamb. James brough the mare home. Fine day.
7. Went to Church Harbour and Cape (illegible). Fine day.
8. Took 14 quarters of mutton to James Hardy.
9. Hewing sleigh runners and after sheep. very cold. day.
10. Working in the shop. cold day
11. Went to a tea meeting in the evening. Fine day.
12. Sawing wood. A very bad snowstorm. Sea went all over the beaches.
13. Splitting wood and shovelling snow.
14. At house road too bad to go to church.
15. Took over three sheep to the Harbour. Two for James one for (illegible)
16. Took three lambs over to D. McGilvary. weather soft andagreeable.
17. Working in the shop. very cold.
18. Mr Abram Hardy and wife came to visit us. fine.
19. Making a sleigh.
20. Drove Mr & Mrs Hardy to the Harbour.
21. Went to church in the evening. a very fine day.
22. Breaking roads. Hardy came to see us
23. Helping Charles Hardy hew a boat bottom.
30. A bad storm of snow and then rain.
31. Breaking the road through the crust.

FEBRUARY

1. Braking the road to the woods. Hauled a load of poles home.
2. Making a pair of moccasins. William Nicholl came.
5. Had a chopping party.
6. Cutting roads and piling wood.fine
7. Commenced hauling wood. fine
8. Helping Zed put in hay, and hauling wood. rain in the night.
9. Took over a tub of butter to James Hardy.
10. Hauling wood. storm in the night
11. At home sick with headache. storm - windy and rough
12. Hauling wood
13. Finished all the wood I had cut. a very cold day
15. Cutting wood at the door and making axe handle. very cold
16. Had MacPherson helping me saw some logs.

There is an old saying that in years of snow, crops will grow. Snow provides some moisture, although ten inches of snow is equivalent to only one inch of rain. Snow has been called the poor man's fertilizer. It doesn't contain appreciable amounts of plant nutrients but it does imporve the texture of the soil and provides for a slow release of moisture in the spring, acting as as a winter mulch and an insulator. A garden rests as comfortably under a snow blanket as a person does under a down comforter and for many of the same reasons.

Many plants and animals have adapted to the effects of extreme cold. But dropping temperatures are not the greatest stress. Wind makes a cold day frigid.

On a winter's night, bright twinkling stars show that the atmosphere is dry and free of clouds. Temperatures may drop sharply, but a storm is not likely. If looking for snow, watch for a halo around the moon and hazy star clusters. If flakes are big there will be only a little snow and it will soon turn to rain. "Little snow, big snow; big snow, little snow."

FEBRUARY

This month is named after Februa - Roman feast of Purification. Gaelic, "Faoilleach" - "Month of Ravaging Wolves"; Anglo/Saxon, "Solmonath" for the cakes were now offered to gods, to rejoice for the return of the sun from its low course in the heavens. Saxons also called it "Sprout-Kale", for the sprouting of kale (cabbage). Micmac "Apuknajit" - "the snow blinder". The full moon is the "Snow Moon".

Come when the rains
Have glazed the snow and clothed the trees with ice,
While slant sun of February pour
Into the bowers a flood of light.
"A Winter Piece" by William Cullen Bryant

February was the purification season falling halfway between the festivals of the Winter Solstice and the Spring Equinox. Fire festivals purified land and livestock. But it was, perhaps, the purification of women that was dominant. The ceremonies revolved around women after childbirth. This was also connected to the rush of milk from the mothers and also from the cattle, who had been dry all winter and now were freshening after spring calving. Juno, queen of the Roman goddesses, was the special protector of women and presided over all aspects of womanly life, especially marriage and childbirth. The moon was believed to control the sexual life and monthly menstrual cycle of a woman. Juno was also worshipped as a moon and fertility goddess and once a year at this time matrons of Rome, carrying torches and candles, made special offerings.

Following Jewish law, Mary, forty days after giving birth to Jesus, presented her baby at the temple. At this time the infant Jesus was prophecied to be "a light". This day, February 2, became known as Candlemas Day, or St. Mary's Feast of the Candles, commemorating the churching or the purification of Mary. It became popular for women, after recovering from childbirth, to carry candles with them as they went to be "churched". Thus the candles that had been blessed were taken home and kept as protection from many things, including sickness. So the candles were for them much as the fragments of the fires had been for their ancient ancestors.

The Celtic St. Bride of England and Scotland, (Bridget of Ireland) also had her festival on this day. She replaced the pagan goddess of marriage, the home and helper of women at childbirth. One legend has Bride being present at Bethlehem to aid Mary in delivering Jesus.

Bride was also connected with fire festivals and the rites of spring. Like the Greek, Persephone, she had been kept prisoner all winter. One legend had her waiting to be rescued by Aengus, the Ever-Young, who lived on a green island of perpetual summer. Another legend had her walking over bleak and desolate land, waving her wand or staff, and causing the growth of new vegetation and flowers.

Bride was associated both with the coming of spring and the end of the harvest. Bride figures or crosses were made of grain and decorated with shells, ribbons, and flowers, and kept all winter. On the eve of St. Bride's day the old Bride figures, which had been kept in houses or in barns all winter to protect them from fire, lightning and sickness, were given to the animals or ploughed into the fields. New figures were made and danced from house to house, with people giving gifts, welcoming and feasting in her honour.

Remnants of these ceremonies were still evident here in Cape Breton into the 1930s. A leader was chosen and, dressed up, he carried a big staff decorated with knots and ribbons. The Chandeleur, as he was known, led men in the community along with two or three carts from house to house singing, dancing and asking for gifts of food. The food was taken to the biggest house in the community for the festivities. Later the community gathered in the house to celebrate until early morning. Home brew, made from molasses, yeast and water, and blueberrry or beet wine for the ladies, were drunk. The breakfast which followed was usually potatoes and pickled mackerel.

Afterwards everyone went to church. People and their candles were blessed. Two lighted candles were crossed and presented in a blessing to a person's throat. This was a reminder of an old custom practised on February 3, St. Blaise's Day. On his day, churches held ceremonies of the blessing of the throat by tying blessed candles into the shape of a cross and touching them against the throats of people with throat ailments. The blessed candles were taken home and used throughout the year and they would be lit if people were sick or when they were being prepared for death.

Candlemas Day, February 2, is also a day to predict weather. In more recent times it has become known as Groundhog Day in North America but in other parts of the world a badger, hedgehog or bear predicts the weather. If he comes out of his winter home and sees his shadow, there will be six more weeks of winter. If the day is cloudy and he sees no shadow, spring will soon be here. The best known ground hog is Pauxatawny Phil who lives in Pauxatawny, Pennsylvania. Festivities surround his annual peek outside.

If Candlemas Day bring snow and rain
Winter is gone, and won't come again.
If Candlemas Day be clear and bright
Winter will have another flight.

February 14, Valentine's Day, is named after St. Valentine. One of the origins of this day, but not the name, is in a spring festival, Lupercalia, celebrated by the ancient Romans every year in mid-February at a site near the Lupercal, or "wolf's grotto", a cave on the western slope of the Palatine Hill. Close by was the fig tree under which the twin infants, Romulus and Remus, the legendary founders of Rome, had been stranded and then found and nursed by a she-wolf. One legend has it that a shepherd found the boys and brought them home for his wife to raise. She had been a whore, known in Latin as a "lupa" or a "she-wolf". In any event, Lupercalia commemorated the founding of the city of Rome and it was the last of the pagan festivals to be given up after the triumph of Christianity.

This festival was a mixture of different festivals honouring similar gods. For example, the Roman god, Faunus, was a nature god, worshipped at this time as guardian and promoter of the fertility of crops, herds, and people. He taught field and animal husbandry. A kindly god of fruitfulness with prophetic powers, he was worshipped, especially by herdsmen.

In the spring rites of purification, goats were sacrificed to ensure that the land and herds would produce, that they would be clean, pure and free from infertility. Faunus was associated with Fauna, his daughter or wife, who was worshipped exclusively by women and with Sabine, another ancient agricultural goddess. Faunus took on the characteristics of the Greek god, Pan, and it is the image and character of Pan that has survived.

Pan was half human and half animal, with a hairy body and the lower limbs of a goat. He is usually pictured wearing a crown made from a pine branch and playing the syrinx (the pipes of Pan), a wind instrument made of different lengths of reeds. He had the goat's prodigious agility and bestial passions. More than any other god he personified instinct. A lusty, playful god, sex was his principal diversion. For his pleasures he pursued nymphs and young boys. Nymphs were originally supernatural creatures who lived in streams, beneath the bark of trees, in the waves of the sea, and on mountains. They were part of the basic fertility pattern in nature.

In ancient times human victims were sacrificed at his festival but later, goats and dogs replaced them. As part of the ceremonies young men, carrying thongs cut from goatskins, ran naked except for belts of animal skins, about the streets lashing everyone they met. The young women wanted to be struck, believing this would make them fruitful and give them an easy delivery. It was an act of purification for both the land and the people. Originally the runners traced a circle around the village, acting simultaneously as wolves surrounding the sheep and as protectors to keep wolves away from the sheep and from the people. The god Pan was both shepherd and protector and wolf and enemy.

Today we think of Pan as a lascivious symbol, "a lecherous old goat". The implications are sexual. We refer to a man who fancies himself with the ladies as a "wolf" and, when a pretty girl walks down the street, some young men give a wolf's whistle.(see also December)

Lotteries were involved in the rites. Originally they selected the human sacrifices, but later they had less terrifying aspects. Each young man drew by lottery the name of a young woman who would share the festivities with him and be his "companion" for the rest of the year.

When Christianity became the principal faith among the Romans, the priests tried to do away with this pagan ritual, but it was almost impossible and the church compromised. Lots were still drawn, but the lottery contained names of saints instead of girls. The young men were asked to imitate the good works of the saint whose name they had drawn. This version was less popular and did not last long.

It is this compromise that brought the name of St. Valentine to the festival day. Valentine was a powerful and popular Roman priest. But he was martyred on February 14 after defying the Emperor. One story has it that the Emperor decided to abolish marriages because husbands made poor soldiers. Valentine believed this was against the laws of God and nature and he continued to perform Christian marriage ceremonies secretly. Discovered, he was sentenced to death and executed. For many generations after it was popular to be married on the day he died, to keep his memory alive.

An old belief that the birds selected their mates on this day has added to the day's being one of courtship and love. Here we also get the terms "billing" and "cooing" from the courtship rituals of the birds.

The old festivals with the new name became very popular in England. The game of choosing valentines was played for years, patterned after the old Roman rite of using the lottery to choose a partner. In some places both the girls and the boys chose a name. The person of the opposite sex would be his or her valentine for a whole year as a sweetheart, lover or friend. The bond was to last a year unless, as one bachelor jokingly put it, "it was terminated by the marriage or death of the partners".

Later on it became the custom for the young people to give their "valentines" a gift. For a man it was usually a pair of gloves if he was serious about the girl. This practice was symbolic of asking for the young lady's hand in marriage. The gloves were made of baby lambskins or kidskins, another part of the Lupercalia festival surviving, although in a different form.

The custom of sending a gift as a valentine was soon changed to sending a message - sayings or verses which the senders themselves wrote. Those who did not want to write their own could always go to books such as the COMPLETE BRITISH VALENTINE WRITER, published in 1797. This book, subtitled the High Road to Love for Both Sexes, contained a complete set of letters and valentines and a variety of pleasing verses calculated "to crown with mirth and good humour the happy day which is called St Valentine, which the youth of both sexes may read without blushing, and those of riper years find much pleasure and entertainment."

Later, with the growing popularity of the custom, ready-made cards were sold. These were usually lacy and delicate, with messages hidden beneath little flaps, or under flower petals or within very complex lovers' knots. Elegant and expensive Victorian cards had silk fringed edges.

Now the day is mostly commercial with emphasis on buying cards, flowers, candy or other gifts. But it is still linked to passions, fertility and the choice of mates.

Winter was the season when men could find work in logging camps. The Oxford Paper and Pulp Company at Murray (near North River Bridge), Cape Breton, in the winter of 1922-23 alone, employed seven hundred men and ran ten logging camps. Over the winter, the men, with the help of one hundred fifty horses and using axes and crosscut saws, cut fifty eight thousand cords of wood. By 1931 the depression in the pulp market ended the operation at the plant and also the wages to choppers of five to ten dollars a day, plus accommodation.

Winter is still the season for colds. Many homemade remedies are perhaps just as valid as some of today's over-the-counter remedies.

Coughs, Colds and Sore Throats:

For coughs, spread goose grease, lard or kerosene on the chest, and cover with wool. Or make an onion poultice - peel, chop, crush and heat and put in a cloth bag on chest.

For a sore throat wrap a wool sock (dirty if possible) around throat; put a little kerosene on the wool.

For coughs, boil and steep like a tea black cherry bark, alder bark, spruce or fir bark. Wine may be added. Drink before bed.

Dried or fresh leaves and flowers of colt's foot make a tea for sore throats and was one of Europe's most popular cough remedies.

Heat one half cup of milk with raisins, and one or two teaspoons of sugar.

Boil comfrey root in water, add equal amount of milk and simmer.

Hot toddy was taken only if you thought you were dying because liquor was precious, and it was believed that "The Lord was the doctor".

Mix fir tips with sugar and water to make an edible jelly.

Roast a lemon, avoid burning it, and cut it into halves and squeeze juice on three tablespoons of powdered maple sugar. Mix and take by the teaspoonful for a cough.

For hot honey lemon tea, add honey and lemon juice to a cup of tea.

Boil molasses, vinegar and butter; or boil molasses and add a small amount of white or Minard's linament or pepper, and cool. Then drink it.

Onions should be eaten boiled or raw twice a week, but may also be shaved and boiled with molasses.

For children's onion syrup slice onions, sprinkle sugar on them, simmer and give a teaspoonful four or five times a day.

Dip a feather in kerosene and swab the throat.

Put cayenne pepper in tea.

Put salt on your tongue or salt mackerel or herring on your feet. An alternative is to rub cloves of garlic on the feet. By the next morning the odor will be up by the nose. If nothing else the smell will help clear sinuses.

Chew a crushed clove of garlic, drink angelica syrup made from the stems or suck candy made of horehound or coltsfoot.

For coughs, thrush, whooping cough or a "tickle" in the throat, a live frog was suspended in the throat so that the cough could be transferred to the frog. When someone with a cough or sore throat mentioned having a "frog in his throat", it was meant literally.

For stuffy noses, sniff milk from a tablespoon.

Cold's best remedy, however, was nutritious chicken soup.

By mid February they said "half the winter/ half the hay", but there were years when the hay had run out by this time and other supplies were low.

The winter of 1904-1905 was a particularly hard one in Nova Scotia. Storms throughout February added to already existing hardships. On farms it was difficult to water the stock. Although sheep get moisture from snow, cattle and horses need water. Often snow had to be melted to provide a sufficient supply.

On Cape Breton supplies of hay were either very low or non-existant. With roads blocked and boats stuck in ice, feed supplies could not reach coastal communities. But with hay having cost less in the fall, many people along the coast had decided to overwinter greater numbers of stock. At the end of February, some relief came to Mira, Gabarus and Louisbourg on the south coast when schooners could once again move with supplies. Other areas were relieved by supplies by road and train, even though one train had been stuck eighteen days at Judique trying to reach Port Hawkesbury. (Today it takes about half an hour by car.) In January, 1917, there was so much snow that it took the Sydney & Louisbourg Railway daily express two days to get the twenty one kilometres from Sydney to Glace Bay.

Communities "Down North", relying on boats to deliver their supplies, suffered hardships somewhat later in the spring as they were accustomed to storing up for the entire winter. However, there were some winters when the bad weather started early in the season when supplies had not all been received.

Rural people were far from supplies. Life was difficult and often there was no money available. People depended on what they grew. When crops were poor or failed, everyone suffered, and some settlements faced starvation. Many have heard of the great potato famine in Ireland in 1846-47, but many in Cape Breton also faced that disaster. Relief was desperately needed in Inverness and Victoria counties. The potato blight in the summer of 1845 left families facing appalling conditions. There was an almost total crop failure. By mid-winter it was impossible to know if existing potatoes would keep and, if they lasted, if they would be good for seed next spring. The summer seemed far away and when faced with starvation people ate what they had, including the seed potatoes.

These conditions continued for the next few years. By midwinter 1848 the future was even bleaker. Famine was imminent. All the seed, potatoes and grain, had been eaten, and cows, calves, and even working cattle had been slaughtered. Many people had no cattle or sheep, nor did they have the means of obtaining seed or food. The few crops planted that summer also failed. To aggravate the situation still further, even the timber business was in a slump.

In part spurred by these conditions, the Reverend Norman McLeod began preparations for the exodus of his community in St. Ann's, Cape Breton, to New Zealand in 1851.

Closer to our own times there have been desperate winters. In 1934, a reporter reached Ingonish by plane and told of desperate conditions. Many were close to starvation. The icebreaker "Montcalm", laden with food and supplies for some three thousand in North Victoria County, tried to smash through solid ice with relief for beleagured fishing villages. Destitute families stole sheep from their more fortunate neighbours. Dairy cows were slaughtered and stores were empty. People existed on a diet of fish and any small game they could trap or hunt. Many children were undernourished and scantily dressed and were suffering from frostbite and impetigo. One resident commented, "I don't suppose you could buy a barrel of flour. If there aren't supplies coming within the next two weeks, there'll be a lot of corpses, because some can't live."

On the other side of the island, the warden of Richmond County set off over snow-covered roads to take an appeal for food to Halifax. Conditions, particularly in Petit de Grat, were reported as critical. Hundreds of people were in immediate need of food. Some families were believed to have been without food for a week. The early freeze-up closed harbours and coves sooner than expected so that fishermen were unable to get their boats to sea. Earlier, the fishing communities had been hit by low prices for fish. Many people pooled their flour to make bread for the children, but now they had run out of everything.

A cloud of despair covered the island.

A tree was once thought to be both a god and where the god lived. When people died they were buried in a hollowed out tree trunk or a tree was planted on their grave. Either way, the belief was that the soul entered the tree, returning to its origin. The modern burial in a wooden coffin derives from this early belief.

To every man upon this earth
Death cometh soon or late.
by Thomas Macaulay

Forerunners, glimpses into the future, are concerned with death. Many believed that if a person dreamed of a knocking at the door, or heard an owl hoot or dogs howl, or the sound of wood being sawn, it meant there would be a death. Or if one dreamt of a wedding, some believed that meant there would soon be a funeral. Another forerunner was dreaming of a funeral procession with a long line of horses and a hearse. As many still do, they said death came in threes. If there is one, there will be two more in the immediate family or neighbourhood.

A hundred or so years ago there remained a few superstitions connecting bees with death. Bees were considered to be as intelligent as humans and became part of the beekeeper's family. They were told of family events. If there was a funeral, a black ribbon was hung from the hive. If it was the beekeeper himself that had died, a member of the family would stand in front of the hive and tell the bees about the death. If this was not done, it was feared the bees would leave.

In England there was a custom of turning the hive around at the moment the beekeeper's body was brought from the house. In other parts, bees were formally invited to the funeral. If a swarm of bees settled on unfamiliar property and were not claimed by their owner, there would be a death in the family within the year.

In many places it is still a custom to touch the dead body. Some say it is to show that you never bore the dead person any ill will. If you had hurt him in life you would not go near him in death, they thought.

Mirrors in a house where a death had occurred were covered with white or black material. This prevented the dead person's image from being seen.

Dead people were waked at home. Friends and family would gather, sit, drink tea and talk about the deceased lying in the open coffin in the same room. This made death more a part of life and therefore not so intimidating. Like the seasons of nature, there are seasons to our lives, ending with death.

The woods decay, the woods decay and fall,
The vapours weep their burden to the ground,
Man comes and tills the field and lies beneath,
And after many a summer dies the swan.
"Tithonus l" by Alfred Lord Tennyson

If Winter comes, can Spring be far behind?
"Ode to the West Wind" by P.B.Shelley

Appendix

SPRING

REPAIRS

Recipe for oil cloths. One pint Chipan. One pint linseed oil boiled. Mix the two liquids together. Rub on the clothes in the morning. By noon it will be dry. Rub on another coat in the evening. Let dry. Guaranteed water-proof. Goose grease is also used to waterproof boots.

PLANKED SALMON

One hardwood plank 8 cm thick, 35-4- cm wide, 90-100 cm long. One salmon 1.5 kg - 3 kg.

Clean the salmon and run a sharp knife along both sides of the backbone so it can be easily removed. Remove head, tail and fins. Remove small bones with pliers.

Sprinkle the inside generously with salt. Close, then leave for a couple of hours

Arrange two stones or bricks about 50-60 cm apart in front of the fire. Stand the plank on its edge to heat. When the plank is hot, place the salmon on it, skin-side down. Use green saplings crisscrossed and nailed at the ends to hold the fish in place.

Sprinkle salmon with flour and stand the plank in front of the fire till brown, allowing 10 minutes per each 3 cm of thickness on the fish. Brush hot butter over the fish before serving.

A DURABLE WHITEWASH

For five gallons - slake six quarts of good lime in hot water; covering it up in the process of slaking, to keep in the steam; when slaked strain through a coarse cloth; add one quart of salt, prepared by boiling in water until dissolved, and the impurities have been skimmed off. To make a brilliant white, to the amount of lime above mentioned, add one quarter pound of burnt alum, one pound of refined sugar, three pounds coppens, three quarters pound of colouring. Applied hot, it will make a very pure white that will last some years.

DANDELION WINE

Take the flower heads, put in a crock, pour one gallon of boiling water over them. Cover and leave for ten days. Stir occasionally. Strain off the flowers. Put liquid in a large pot. Add four pounds sugar. Peel and slice one orange and lemon and add to liquid. Boil for twenty minutes and return to the crock. When cool, spread one yeast cake on a slice of toast and add. Cover and leave for two days. Put in a five gallon cask and cork. Let it ferment two months, then bottle. That's the hard part - waiting those two months.

SUMMER

LEMONADE

Syrup - boil one cup sugar and two cups of water for five minutes. Add one third cup of lemon juice, cool and dilute to taste.

One quart - one half cup each of sugar and lemon juice to three and one quarter cups of water.

CLOVER HONEY

Dry flower heads a couple of days, pour boiling water over them, let steep.

5 cups sugar, 1 1/2 cups water, 1/4 tsp. powdered alum. Boil. Mix for 5 minutes. Pour the syrup over 40 white clover heads, 20 red clover heads, 3 rose petals. Let stand 20 minutes. Strain syrup and bottle.

LOST AGRICULTURE

The listing of the categories at an Agricultural and Industrial Exhibition at Mabou in October, 1887, demonstrates the variety of agricultural life and the self-sufficiency of the people. It also illustrates the extent to which much of the past has been lost.

There was a wider class and breed listing, some rarely seen today. Cattle: best herd and individual animals thoroughbred Ayshires, Durhams, Devons, Guernseys, Jerseys, Holsteins, Polled Angus, Herefords, and grade cattle and oxen.

Sheep: Shropshire Downs, Southdowns, long wool Leicesters, Cotswolds, grades & crosses.

Swine: Berkshires, Yorkshire or Ellsmeres, White Chesters

Poultry: turkeys, geese, ducks, hens and chickens - Brahma, Cochin, Spanish, Leghorn, Plymouth Rock, Hamburg

Best crock of butter, not less than ten pounds; best butter in rolls or prints, best dairy cheese.

Best sheaf of red spring wheat, winter wheat, buckwheat, barley, white oats, black oats, new & improved oats, Indian corn, as well as displays of field peas and horse beans

Best flour, certified to have been made from wheat grown in Cape Breton, not less than fifty pounds. And best loaf of bread from Cape Breton Island flour.

Apples: Gravensteins, Nonpareil, Northern Spy, Ribstone Pippins, Rhode Island Greening, Baldwins, Golden Russets, Red Astrachan, White Astrachan, Tamieuse, Duchess of Oldenburg. Crab apples: Siberian Crab, Transcendant Crab, Queen's Choice, Red Hyslop or Montreal Beauty. A variety of plums: White Magnum Bonum, Red Magnum Bonum, Blue, Greengages, White, Damsons, Arctic, as well as several varieties of pears, along with grapes and cranberries.

Farm self-sufficiency was demonstrated with the following items: Best double iron harness, ox yoke - complete with bows, fanning mill, field roller, horse cart-two wheels, ox cart, garden wheelbarrow, stump lifter, farm gate, cart wheels, horse shoes for summer use, for winter use, grubbing hoe and potato hoe.

Best bundle sawn shingles, split shingles, panel door, window sash, extension or centre table of native wood, best piece of furniture, fish barrel, pork barrel, nest butter tubs-softwood, axe handles, pick handles, shovel handles, truck waggon (double), family carriage, buggy, express waggon, double sleigh, single sleigh, small spinning wheel, power churn.

Leather work: best double or single truck harness, double or single carriage harness, riding saddle and martingale, side grained neats leather, side waxed leather, grained or waxed calf skins, trunk, hand valise.

There were collections of cloths: all wool, dressd or undressed, power loom, all wool, dressed & fulled (coloured), hand loom; women's wear, plain or fancy pattern, hand loom; white flannel, all wool; cotton and wool; pair blankets, hand loom; hearth rug - all native wool or rag or braided; best carpet,all wool or rag; best men's woolen socks or stockings or mitts or gloves; knitting yarn, white or coloured- hand spun; men's knitted undershirts or drawers or Guernseys; women's shawl; flax table cloth or towelling, linen sheeting; two or more straw hats; sheepskin mats; patchwork or crazy quilts; counterpane.

Canned goods included preserves, pickles, vegetables and salmon and lobster.

Other classes at the Cape Breton County Exhibition also included: fish classes: best half quintal of codfish, haddock, or pollack, best exhibit of boneless codfish; best half barrel No. 1 mackerel or No. 1 herring; best twenty pounds of green codfish; best two boxes of smoked herring; best half dozen finnan haddie; best twenty pounds smoked halibut; best model fishing schooner and best collection of fish.

Indian work included best assortment market & clothes baskets; ladies or work basket; best pair of beaded moccasins; best six axehandles, or three hockey sticks; best alder setee, lobster trap, assortment of baskets

INVERNESS PRODUCES

In 1880 Inverness was the province's leading county in agricultural productivity. There were 5,558 horses, a greater number than any other county in Nova Scotia. There were more livestock: 29,843 cattle, 458 working oxen, 45,453 sheep and 5,573 swine. There was more wool: 117,081 pounds of wool; as well as 649,276 pounds of butter, 158,000 pounds of cheese, 9,549 pounds of flax and 147,811 yards of homemade cloth and flannel, 5,788 yards of linen, 5,668 pounds of maple sugar and 3,730 bushels of apples were produced, only the later being small compared to the Valley's production.

FALL

MINCEMEAT

5 pounds boiled beef or tongues, 6 pounds peeled apples, 2 1/2 pounds suet, 3 pounds raisins, 2 pounds currants, 1/2 pound each of chopped citron, candied orange and lemon peel, 4 pounds sugar, 1 tbsp each of cinnamon, allspice, cloves, nutmeg and salt, 1/2 pound of grated/chopped almonds, rind & juice of 4 oranges & 4 lemons, and brandy & whisky

Cook the meat. After it is cool, chop fine and add sugar, raisins, currants, citron. Mix. Finely chop apples and add to the meat. Add the spices and mix. Pour over the mixture one quart of brandy and two quarts of whisky, add rind and juice of oranges and lemons.

Put in an earthern crook with a lid. Place a cloth over the top and then put on the lid. Keep in a cool place for about 3 weeks. If you wish add more salt and spices. Let stand another 4 weeks before using. Then place in glass Mason jars or keep covered with cheesecloth in the cool barn for the winter. (BUTCHERING, PROCESSING AND PRESERVATION OF MEAT by Frank G. Ashbrook)

ROSE GERANIUM JELLY

2 and 1/2 cups water   6 and 1/2 cups sugar   1 cup liquid pectin

Put sugar and water into large saucepan. Add pink colouring to give desired shade. Add several rose geranium leaves. Stir and bring to boiling point. Add pectin, boil 1 minute. Take from fire, let stand 1 minute, skim, remove geranium leaves, pour quickly, and cover hot jelly at once with hot paraffin wax. Paraffin again when cold. For a tart jelly, add the juice of 1 lemon to above recipe. If lemon flavor is desired, add also the grated lemon rind.

BRINE

There is a "dry" cure or brine. A brine is made by adding coarse salt to water, along with sugar or honey, saltpeter, which gives the hams the pink colour, and various spices. The meat is left in this brine. Hams and shoulders are usually kept there for four days per pound, so that, for example, a fifteen pound ham needs about sixty days in the brine. Small four to six pound picnic hams need twenty five to thirty days, bacon only needs one and a half to two days per pound. So called "Canadian bacon", a prized lean cut of meat, is made by cutting the loin section out and rolling it before curing.

TO RENDER LARD

Fat renders more rapidly and yields a higher percentage of lard if first cut into small uniform pieces. Cooking should be very slow until the fat melts and can be stirred. Then the heat is raised a little. The crackling (crisp skin, or rind, of the cooked pork) turns light brown and floats. Many people stop cooking the fat when the cracklings are still floating, others leave them until they sink to the bottom. This lard will keep better. The cracklings are dried and eaten. Lard was held to be an excellent ingredient in pastry and in certain types of cooking.

SOAP

A combination of tallow and lard made the best soap. Poultry fats and vegetable oils were combined with other fats, as soap solely from them was too soft and spongy. Sometimes the fat smelled badly but lost some of its odour when boiled in lye.

Waste fat needed to be clarified: melted slowly and strained through two thicknesses of cheesecloth. Then an equal amount of hot water was added and brought to a boil. It was then removed from the fire. After constant stiring and the addition of cold water the fat was set aside to cool. When firm, the clean fat on top was ready to make into soap. Fat stripped from the intestines of pigs, sheep, and cattle after butchering and fat from corned beef and fried pork after eating was saved.

Other materials needed to make soap were borax, lye and soft (rain) water. Borax improved the appearance and "sudsing" of the soap. Care had to be taken with lye, a caustic acid.

Early settlers made their own lye from wood ash. A barrel was suspended over a tub and ashes from the kitchen stove were saved in the barrel. Water was poured over the ashes and the mixture, left to settle, gradually dripped into the tub.

The ingredients were put in a big enamel, iron or earthenware pot on an outside fire and stirred with a wooden paddle.

When the lye got hot and started to boil, it split the fats. A long handled dipper and a few drops of cold water helped control the boiling. A drop of the liquid was put in a cup of water and if it solidified like fudge, the soap was done. It had a straw or molasses candy color to it.

The year's supply was good for washing and scrubbing. There were lots of suds which would take the stains out of anything. Wood floors and diapers came out white as snow.

Molds for soap were made from cardboard, wooden boxes or shallow enamel pans which could be lined with waxed paper or with cotton cloth. The thickened soap mixture was poured into molds, covered and kept warm for about twenty four hours. The soap was removed, cut into bars and aged for two weeks. Some soap was just kept in a pot in the milkhouse. Though good for washing clothes homemade soap was too harsh for personal use and that soap had to be purchased.

CANDLES

This tallow was also boiled and poured into molds. Early settlers often put the molds in snowbanks to freeze. When taken back into the house the candles would come easily from the molds. Often different fragrances were added to the tallow which would be released when the candles burned.

HUNTING

Other game allowed to be hunted in the late 1800s were partridge, woodcock, snipe, teal, blue-winged duck and wood duck. Hunters could catch pheasants, spruce partridge, blackcock, sharp-tailed grouse, rabbits and hares. Animals incuded in the hunt were beaver, mink, bear, wolf, loupcervier (Canadian lynx), wildcat, skunk, musquash (black bear), raccoon, fox, wodchuck, otter and weasel.

WINTER

THE WINTER PANTRY

Even less than a hundred years ago a typical pantry might include close to two hundred pounds of flour, a bagful each of oatmeal, cornmeal and whole wheat. In addition there would be five gallons of kerosene, two of molasses, ten pounds of sugar, some cream of tartar and baking soda, and about ten pounds of tea in a box lined with foil. A luxury was MacDonald's Twist smoking tobacco and Navy tobacco that had to be cut with a knife and kneaded before being smoked.

HAGGIS

Mix ground liver and kidneys of sheep with suet, oatmeal, onion, salt and pepper, and boil in a casing for several hours. Maragh is a meatless haggis.

SILIBUB

1 cup wine	2 cups milk
1 quart cream	1 cup sugar.

Mix ingredients and beat well. Serve only the foam, sprinkled with nutmeg.

WASSAIL

The component parts of wassail are ale, sugar, nutmeg, and roasted apples.

Grated nutmeg	2 tsps cinnamon
2 cloves	2 bottles wine(claret,
1 tsp. ginger	sauterne or burgandy)
blade of mace	1 lb. sugar
1 tsp allspice	12 eggs
12 hot baked apples	

Put the spices in 1/2 cup of water and bring to a boil. Add the wine and heat. Add sugar. Beat separately yolks and whites of eggs. Fold yolks into beaten whites and put in punch bowl. Pour the warm spiced wine over the eggs and beat till frothy - this gave it the appearance and nickname of "lamb's wool". While liquid is foaming, add the hot baked apples.

MILK DESSERT

Pour cream into cups and cover tops with a cloth. Leave the cups for 24 hours until the cream thickens. Then pour on maple syrup or sugar.

CHICKEN SOUP

1 broiler chicken, whole or cut up.	1 tbsp vinegar
1/2 tsp pepper	1 bay leaf
3/4 c chopped onions	1/2 cup chopped cabbage
1/2 c. chopped celery	5 cups cold water
3/4 c chopped green pepper	1 1/2 tsp salt
1 can (16 oz) tomatoes	1 tsp chopped parsley
1 1/2 tsp each of tarragon and basil.	

In large saucepan place chicken with cold water, and spices. Bring to a boil, cover and simmer 1 1/2 - 2 hours or until meat falls off bones. Pour off broth, strain and refrigerate to separate from fat. When chicken is cool, remove bones and skin and chop chicken into bite size pieces. Skim fat from refrigerated broth and melt in bottom of saucepan. Saute onions, celery and green pepper for 5 min. Add tomatoes, vinegar, bay leaf, broth and chopped cabbage. Simmer 10 min. Add chicken and heat.

SELECTED BIBLIOGRAPHY

Agricultural and Industrial Exhibition Prize List. Mabou. Oct 11-13, 1887. Pam. 3527. Beaton Institute, Sydney, NS

Arthur, Mildred H. HOLIDAYS OF LEGEND. Harvey House, New York 1971

Ashbrook, Frank G. Butchering, PROCESSING AND PRESERVATION OF MEATS. Van Nostrand Reinhold Co. New York. 1955 copyright by Litton Educational Publishing Co.

Bauval, Robert & Adrian Gilbert. THE ORION MYSTERY. Doubleday Canada Ltd. Toronto 1996. Orginally published in Great Britain by William Heinemann Ltd & in the United States by Crown Publishers Inc, 1994

BLUE BOOKS FOR NOVA SCOTIA, Vols 44-76 en passim. 1820-30 combined with Nova Scotia statistics

BLUENOSE MAGIC. ed. by Helen Creighton. The Ryerson Press, Toronto 1968

Boxer, Arabella & Philippa Back. THE HERB BOOK. Octopus Books Ltd. London 1980

Burne, Charlotte Sophia. THE HANDBOOK OF FOLKLORE. Sidgwick & Jackson Ltd. London 1913 (This edition - Senate, an imprint of Studio Editions Ltd. London 1995)

Calder, Nigel. THE COMET IS COMING! The Viking Press, New York 1980

Cape Breton Magazine. en passim. in particular. Sophie Deveau of Cheticamp; Marguerite Gallant of La Pointe & Joe Delaney of St Joseph du Moine (feast of Chandeleur); Dave Epstein, Sydney; Hattie Carmichiel; Roderick MacLeod & his neighbours on the North Shore for "Oidche Na Calluinn"; John Alex John X MacDonald & his neighbours on the North Shore for milling frolics. ed. by Ron Caplan, Wreck Cove, Nova Scotia

Chambers, R. THE BOOK OF DAYS. 2 vols. London & Edinburgh 1866

CONSUMPTION: Its Cause, Prevention, and Cure. ed. by George H. Cox & John W. MacLeod. Issued by the Tri-County Anti-Tuberculosis League of Antigonish, Guysborough and Pictou, Nova Scotia. 1911

Cooper, J.C. DICTIONARY OF SYMBOLIC & MYTHOLOGICAL ANIMALS. Thorsons. An imprint of Harper Collins Publishers, London 1995. (first published by The Aquarian Press as Symbolic and Mythological Animals 1992)

Croft, Peter. ROMAN MYTHOLOGY. Octopus Books Ltd. London 1974

D'Andrea, Jeanne. ANCIENT HERBS. The J. Paul Getty Museum, Malibu, Ca. 1982

Diamond, Denise. LIVING WITH FLOWERS. Quill, New York 1980

Donaldson, Elizabeth & Gerald. THE BOOK OF DAYS. A & W Publishers Inc, New York 1979 by arrangement with Jonathan-James Books, Toronto

Eliot, Alexander. MYTHS with contributions by Mircea Eliade & Joseph Campbell. McGraw-Hill Co., New York, St Louis, San Francisco, Montreal, New Delhi, Sao Paulo, Singapore, Toronto 1975. (copyright McGraw-Hill Book Co. (Ltd), Maidenhead, England)

ENCYCLOPEDIA OF NEWFOUNDLAND & LABRADOR. Vol. I. First Edition. "Christmas Customs" by Wayne C. Stockwood. editor in chief Joseph R. Smallwood. Newfoundland Book Publishers Ltd, St. John's 1967

A FAMILY CHRISTMAS. The Reader's Digest Association, Pleasantville, New York 1984

Ferguson, Sandra. On Herbs. Fortress of Louisbourg National Historic Park 1976

Foster, Steven & James A. Duke. A FIELD GUIDE TO MEDICINAL PLANTS IN EASTERN & CENTRAL NORTH AMERICA. The Peterson Field Guides. Houghton Mifflin & Co., Boston 1990

Gottfried, Robert S. THE BLACK DEATH. The Free Press, A division of Macmillan Publishing Co, Inc. New York, N.Y. 1983

Haliburton, T.C. HISTORY OF NOVA SCOTIA, Vol. II. Halifax 1829

Hancock, Graham. FINGRPRINTS OF THE GODS. Seal Books. McClelland-Bantam, Inc. Toronto 1996 (first published in Great Britain by William Heinemann Ltd 1995)

Hartley, Dorothy. LOST COUNTRY LIFE, Pantheon Books, New York 1979

Helfman, Elizabeth S. MAYPOLES AND WOOD DEMONS. The Seabury Press, New York 1972

THE HOLY BIBLE, Revised Standard Version. William Collins Sons & Co., Ltd, New York, Glascow & Toronto 1952

Howell, Frank. Exports from Cape Breton 1797-1865

THE ILLUMINATED BOOK OF DAYS. ed. by Kay & Marshall Lee. Macdonald & Jane's Publishers Ltd. London 1979

Inverness County Statistics, quoted in North Sydney Herald April 9, 1884

Inwards, Richard. WEATHER LORE. Elliot Stock, London 1893 this edition-Senate, an imprint of Studio Editions Ltd. London 1994

Kightly, Charles. THE PERPETUAL ALMANACK OF FOLKLORE. Thames and Hudson. London 1987. (First published in United States by Thames and Hudson, Inc N.Y. 1987)

Knowlson, T. Sharper. THE ORIGINS OF POPULAR SUPERSTITIONS AND CUSTOMS. T. Werner Laurie Ltd. London 1930

LAROUSSE WORLD MYTHOLOGY. edited by Pierre Grimal. The Hamlyn Publishing Group Ltd. London (etc) 1965

Llewellyn's MOON SIGN BOOK & LUNAR PLANTING GUIDE. 1991. Llewellyn Publications, St. Paul, Mn. 1991

Llewellyn's 1991 MAGICKAL ALMANAC. ed. by Raymond Buckland. Llewellyn Publications, St. Paul, Mn. 1991

Mackay, Charles. EXTRAORDINARY POPULAR DELUSIONS AND THE MADNESS OF CROWDS. Wordsworth Reference. Wordsworth Editions Ltd, Hertfordshire, England 1995

MacLeod, Heather & Barbara MacDonald. EDIBLE WILD PLANTS OF NOVA SCOTIA. Nova Scotia Museum. Halifax, NS. 1977

THE MEANING OF GARDENS. History of the Garden Book. ed. by Mark Francis & Randolph T. Hester, Jr. The MIT Press, Cambridge, Ma. 1990

Newton, Pamela. THE CAPE BRETON BOOK OF DAYS. UCCB Press, Sydney 1984

Nohl, Johannes. THE BLACK DEATH. Ballantine Books, Inc. New York, N.Y. 1960

Old Customs of June. Cape Breton Post. Sydney, NS Sept 13, 1930

Ovid, THE METAMORPHOSES. translated freely into verse by Henry T. Riley, G. Bell and Sons Ltd., London 1915

Patten, Helen Philbrook. THE YEAR'S FESTIVALS. Dana Estes & Co. Boston, Ma. 1903

Patterson's HISTORY OF VICTORIA COUNTY. ed. by W. James MacDonald. College of Cape Breton Press, Sydney, NS 1978

Pennick, Nigel. THE PAGAN BOOK OF DAYS. Destiny Books, Rochester, Vt. 1992

Ridpath, Ian. STAR TALES. Universe Books, New York 1988

Rohde. Eleanour Sinclair. THE OLD ENGLISH HERBALS. Dover Publications, Inc. New York 1971 (from the work originally published by Longmans, Green & Co. 1922)

Root, Waverly. FOOD. Simon & Schuster, New York 1980

Shaudys, Phyllis. THE PLEASURE OF HERBS. A Garden Way Publishing Book. Storey Communications, Inc. Pownal, Vt. 1986

Sloane, Eric. THE SEASONS OF AMERICA PAST. Wilfred Funk, Inc. New York 1958

Tannahill, Reay. FOOD IN HISTORY. Stein & Day Publishers, New York 1973

Tester, S.J. A HISTORY OF WESTERN ASTROLOGY. Ballantine Books, New York 1987

van Rentergham, Tony. WHEN SANTA WAS A SHAMAN. Llewellyn Publications. St. Paul, Mn. 1995

van Straalen, Alice. THE BOOK OF HOLIDAYS AROUND THE WORLD. E.P. Dutton, New York 1986

Velikovsky, Immanuel. AGES IN CHAOS. Abacus Edition by Sphere Books Ltd., London 1973 (first published in Great Britain by Sidgwick & Jackson Ltd 1953)

Velikovsky, Immanuel. EARTH IN UPHEAVAL. Dell Publishing Co. Inc. New York 1955. Reprinted by arrangement with Doubleday & Co., Inc. New York

Velikovsky, Immanuel. WORLDS IN COLLISION. Abacus Edition by Sphere Books Ltd, London 1972 (first published in Great Britain by Victor Gollancz Ltd 1950)

Wilson, C. Anne. FOOD AND DRINK IN BRITAIN. Constable & Co., Ltd. London 1973

INDEX

PHOTO CREDITS:

SPRING

SUMMER

FALL

WINTER